SOME
WISE WORDS
YOU MAY HAVE
MISSED!!!

SOME
WISE WORDS
YOU MAY HAVE
MISSED!!!

A Second Chance For You

RICHARD G. RIEDEL

ARCHWAY PUBLISHING

Archway Publishing books may be ordered through booksellers or by contacting:

Archway Publishing
1663 Liberty Drive
Bloomington, IN 47403
www.archwaypublishing.com
844-669-3957

ISBN: 978-1-6657-4911-4 (sc)
ISBN: 978-1-6657-4910-7 (e)

Library of Congress Control Number: 2023915889

Print information available on the last page.

Archway Publishing rev. date: 08/23/2023

CONTENTS

THE WHY OF THIS BOOK

In his Book "Help Is Here," Max Lucado captures my reason for this book with these words: "When you sense the Spirit has an important message for you to share, share it! Don't assume that people already know what you know. God might very well be using you to convey an important truth . . . ."

The are so many wonderful truths floating around in this world of ours that we will miss because we did not read them ourselves. I read a lot and have many ideas excited in my mind that feel other people need to know about. They are lost in the books that are published every day, month and year. I have determined to note some of these truths and share them with those who might miss them.

During my Seminary Training we were instructed in a variety of "preacher arts," such as Old And New Testament Exegesis, and finding resources for our weekly presentations by reading widely and regularly.

On Sunday morning we were then able to stand in our pulpits, and share with our listeners, what we had seen in the passages that we selected as the basis for our Sunday morning message.

Each week was a "start over time" for each of our listeners. They heard what we had to say in the context of their past experiences and were invited to hear the message of the day and apply it to their lives. The question that they were asked to consider was "with the information being shared, can you begin to live your life in a new way?"

To read a book involves more than just reading the words the author puts before you. It asks that we understand what the words say to us, and to the world around us. Hopefully, as you read these reflections, they will assist you in traveling along life's road, and in the process, see all there is to see!

HOW TO READ THIS BOOK

This book will take you, very likely, on a three month adventure. Yes, that's right! It will take you at least three months to successfully read through the pages of this book.

We are advised on the pages of the internet, by Fisher Investments, Charles Schwab, and others, and by a host of Business Channels, on how to prepare financely for the years ahead of us. However, we are on our own to prepare ourselves mentally for the next stage in our lives, whether it be for Pretirement, Retirement or Post Retirement.

This book offers you the opportunity to reflect on a host of questions that you can use to percolate your present life through, and prepare you to successfully make plans for your future.

However, that will take some time. Reading each segment of the book, and thinking about the stories and thoughts of wisdom they prepose, will give you the opportunity to "get ready" for your tomorrows

ONE
In The Beginning

I gave a friend a copy of my first book. After reading a number of Reflections he said to me, "You sure have a lot of quotations!

He was right. The book is filled with the words of others. They are there for a reason. In fact they are the reason for the writing of the book.

I do a lot of reading and over the years I have come across a great deal of the wisdom of others. They have said things that often summarize, in a more perfect way, things that I have thought. As I have come across their words I have found in them, truths that I do not want to forget.

I had a Doctor friend in one of the Churches that I served who was a fan of Bartlet's Book Of Familiar Quotations. He would call me on Sunday afternoon and review the words of those whom I had quoted in the Morning Sermon: to correct me or to laud me. The words, phrases or paragraphs that I had written or write about would find their place in "My" Book of quotations.

I need to write these words down and allow them to summarize or explain things that I have thought as I read them. I understand myself better as I find myself explained in the writings of another.

I recently came across these words of Bob Goff: "Take notes while you read this or any other book. Write down how you are going to apply the parts that make sense to you. If you don't net those butterflies immediately, I promise that they will fly away. Do this, then study and refine those notes, and you will find connections between the ideas you have scribbled down in the middle of the conversation and ones you had in other conversations. You will capture meaningful, partially developed and applicable ideas you can incorporate into your life. As you use what you have written down, they will create a feedback loop as they evolve into fuller, more complete ideas. If you don't take the time to capture and process your interior world, you will miss the opportunity to discover something bigger and more beautiful in your heart."

My suggestion to you is, as you read and are confronted by one word or thought or another, in your reading, write them down; think them through and you will find yourself the richer for it.

You are smarter than you think you are! Sometimes all that you have to do is reflect on your thoughts as they are expressed in the writings of another. They will give you a new insight into what you have been thinking.

Again, in the words of Bob Goff: "A life without reflection is a vapor."

TWO

In Search Of Hope and Assurance

Covid 19! Lockdown! Shutdown! Isolation! Political anxiety! Wear a mask. Stay six feet apart! The death of friends and neighbors. Where did they get the virus? Who had it? Who has it? Where is it? It is a silent, invisible enemy. How do you begin the day with confidence? How do you close your eyes at night?

I came upon a story, found in a book written by a renowned writer of devotional literature. The writer, Hannah Whiteall Smith. The book, "Living Confidently In God's Love." The author said that at the time she was experiencing some terrible pains and was faced with some unanswered questions. She was told that there was a woman, staying nearby, who was a deeply spiritual Christian. She was urged to go and meet with the woman, to help her get through her trouble. So, she wrote, "One day I summoned up enough courage and went to see her. I was sure," she noted, 'that the woman would take a deep interest in me, and would take some of her time, to listen to my problems, and give me some answers to them.

Smith writes that the woman listened patiently to me, did not interrupt me, but when I was through with my story, and I paused, expecting her to respond in sympathy and consideration, she simply said, "Yes, all you say may be very true, but then, in spite of it all, there is God.

Smith said that she waited, expecting her to say something else, but nothing came. It was if she had said all that needed to be said, and she was done. "But. I continued, "You don't understand how very serious and perplexing my situations are."

"Oh, yes, I do", she replied. "But then as I tell you, there is God."

I could not induce her to make one more answer. "It seemed to me most disappointing and unsatisfactory. I felt that my peculiar and really harrowing experiences could not be met by anything so simple and so mere as the statement, 'Yes, but there is God.!'"

Later, Ms Smith said, "(But) . . from wondering, I came gradually to believe that being my Creator and Redeemer, He must be enough. And at last, a conviction burst upon me that He really was enough. My eyes were opened to the fact of the absolute and utter sufficiency of God."

"It was a wonderful story and I understood what the woman was saying. The question was: 'Did I believe it?' I wanted to, but did I really believe it? In the face of all of my personal situations did I believe it? I spoke the answer to myself again. "Yes, but there is God." I have shared those words, in one form or another, with countless others, but now, today, when I need to hear it myself, I wonder, do I believe it? Really believe it?

"Yes, I do." But be as it may, the statement continues to haunt me. "Yes, but there is God!" Friends, God has to be enough. He is enough! We just need to wrap our lives around those words.

THREE
Life Begins Anew For Us Everyday!

In a book entitled "In Conversation," Theologian Stanley Hauerwas, now retired, said to his conversational partner, Samuel Wells, now vicar of St. Martins in-the-Fields, London, "When you retire you can hear your power leaving because you no longer, by your very existence, demand attention. And you have to get used to what it means to be not in the forefront anymore. . . . That you lose power. It means what you write, no one needs to read again. There is a loss in that, and you can mourn it, but I suspect it is also a good thing for you to learn how to recognize you're no longer who you once were when you had a job." (1)

It was an experience that I did not have to face until quite late in my life, as my second and third careers lasted until rather late in my life. But I still faced the situation. What do you do when you are "out there," quite alone with yourself. One of the important things to remember in life, is "that we are never alone. Someone is always watching us and listening to us.

It seems to me that one has to ask of themselves, several questions. First, "What was I born to be?" And second, "Who was I born to touch?" Being and touching are always a part of our lives. I am not sure that "being" ever changes. We are what we are, every day, always. However, who we touch,- life makes that determination for us.

And add to that, this thought by A. W Tozer: "One thing that sometimes bothers me is that to some people, I will be the only Bible they will ever read, so to speak." . . "To some people I will be the only expression of Christ's love that they will ever experience." Wow!

In my later years, just after my retirement, I was put in contact with a layperson, who I believe to be one of the most Christian of all the people I have ever known. He brought me face to face with what I ought to be: to look in the mirror and see how I compared myself to him. That view has kept me on guard for all of the years since I have known him, and though I have moved far away from him, I will always remember him, and his example will always be in front of me. Always touching me!

In the last several years I have come in contact with another man. Like the first, he is a layman. He keeps me awake to the possibilities in my life by what he says to me; through our conversations. He reminds me, from time to time, "what reality is all about" and demands, at least in my mind, what I need to be thinking about and what I should be doing.

The lesson to be learned is "Who is looking at me?" and "Who is listening to what I say?" Frankly, those are some very scary questions, with infinite possibilities. Wow! This means, in my mind, that life is new every day: that I am facing new people with new needs, every day.

FOUR

The Importance of KNOWING What You Believe

During my retirement years I am, more often than not, reading three books at a time, each day. Perhaps, it is not a good habit, but I am doing it. It is amazing how many times I find several of the books being in conversation with one another.

For example, today I find myself reading a book, authored by a man by the name of Donald Miller entitled. "Blue Lake Jazz." In a chapter entitled "Belief" I found these words: "What people believe is important." In the same chapter, he had these thoughts: "Can you imagine what Americans would do if they understood over half the world was living in poverty? Do you think they would change the way they live, the products they purchase, and the politicians they elect? If we believed the right things, the true things, there wouldn't be very many problems on earth.." Wasn't it John Paul Sarte who said, somewhere, "All we are is the sum of our actions." Miller concluded: "But the trouble with deep belief is that is costs something. And there is something inside me, some selfish beast of a subtle thing that doesn't like the truth at all because it carries responsibility, and if I actually believed these things I would have to do something. So it is cumbersome to believe anything. And it isn't cool . . . ."

I wonder, what do you believe? "What people believe is important". What people believe is more important than how they look, what their skills are, or their degree of passion. Passion about nothing is like pouring gasoline in a car without wheels. It isn't going to lead anybody anywhere." What do you believe?

That very same afternoon, in reading Senator Rand Paul's book, "The Case Against

Socialism", I came across these words: ". . "Even the most ardent climate change alarmists acknowledge that this debate (between socialism and capitalism) is more than pollution or temperature changes. To many climate activists, it's really about replacing capitalism with socialism.."

"The scientific consensus is that the planet can only be saved by eliminating capitalism." Paul went on to say: ". . climate scientists recently had to admit that their predictions 'contained more errors that made their conclusions seem more certain than they really are."

Now I do not know what I really believe about climate change, whether I am for it or against it, but after thinking through what Miller has written. I now know I had better keep my mouth shut until I really know what I believe. The same holds true for any other issue, political or social, or even what I believe about many sports issues. What do you "really" believe? My advice:: Keep your mouth shut and your opinions to yourself, until you: "really" know.

By the way: if you ever begin to think about "Climate Change", you might want to begin by studying the writings of geophysicist and astronomer Milutin Milankovich, and explore his insights about "Three Reasons" to explore the three main causes of geologic climate change, in the 1920's. To this day, no science has disproved them. I know, that is where I would start.

FIVE

The Importance of knowing WHOM YOU BELIEVE IN

It was, as I was reading a book by Kyle Idelman entitled "God's At War;" in the light of what I wrote earlier: "that it is important that you know what you believe in," that I was stopped by these words: "From the time we're born and introduced to milk we are forever pursuing what we think will satisfy our appetites."

The end result, of course, is that "our lives begin to take the shape of what we care about most. We each make the choice (of whom we want) to worship, and then at some point we discover that that is the choice that makes us.. The object of (our) worship will determine (our) future and define (our) life. It's the one choice that all other choices are motivated by."

Idleman says, what the Old Testament Leader, Joshua said to the children of Israel: "Choose for yourselves this day whom you will serve." He is saying, Idleman writes, we "make an educated decision on the great goal of our life. Otherwise you will passively flow into some choice by mere osmosis, a little bit of you at a time, until you find yourself inside a temple, bowing to a god you never consciously met." We are reminded of the words of John Paul Sarte,: "All we are is the sum of our actions."

The preacher in me makes me make this determination: What you believe in is determined by whom you believe in." Idleman, who is also a preacher, writes: "It's called the "law of exposure. The basic premise is that our lives are determined by our thoughts, and our thoughts are determined by what we are exposed to. The law of exposure means that our minds absorb and our lives ultimately reflect whatever we are most frequently exposed to."

What I guess I am saying here is that you had better stop here and determine, for yourself, "Whom You Believe In?" WHO DO YOU BELIEVE IN?

Let me ask that question of you, once more, because your very life depends upon your answer: "WHO DO YOU BELIEVE IN?" Are you sure that's what you really believe? Really?

SIX

Live Your Life One Day At A Time

I saw it once on a television commercial.. I have not seen it since, - but I saw it once. These words: "Every Thing You Have Been Makes You What You Are." Whatever Ad writer coined those words they must have, at some point in time, been confronted by the words of John Paul Sarte which have been mentioned on earlier pages: "All we are is the sum of our actions." Novelist and poet Madeleine L'Engle made this comment: "The great thing about getting older is that you don't lose all the other ages you've been." And a preacher by the name of Brian D. McLaren added: "The great thing about a new stage is that you get to keep what you learned and became in previous stages."

In her book "A Short History Of Myth," Karen Armstrong makes the point that everytime humans take a step forward, they revise and update their understanding of the world. We are always growing. Armstrong is quoted, along with many others, in a great writing by Bruce Feiler, which he entitled "Life Is In The Transitions." Feiler goes on to remind us of the wisdom of William Shakespeare, found is a speech quoted in his writing in "As You Like It."

> "All the world's a stage.,
> and all the men and women merely players;
> They have their exits and their entrances.
> And one man in his time plays many parts,
> His acts being seven ages."

Feiler suggests that eventually humankind adopted the belief that "life proceeds through a series of ages, phases or stages. It was the writer Gail Sheehy who popularized the concept of the linear life.

The point of it all is that we are, time wise, always involved in the journey we call "our lives." Every second, hour and every day we live, is part of what or who we are, and we should never forget that. Every activity is written down in the book of life. We can't get away from that, nor can we avoid it, or erase it from its place.

The very seconds that you spend reading these words are marks on the parchment of your life; you can't erase them. Do you have something else you ought to be doing, now, instead of reading these words? What might you miss because of it? Think about it. Your life is very important "to you." Every second counts! You are in the process of becoming a new you! Shouldn't you get on with it? RIGHT NOW!

SEVEN

Hope: Never Leave Home Without It!

A good many years ago, now, when I first began to read the newly minted espionage novels, periodically, when the documented hero found his life on the line, I would move ahead to the final pages of the book, to see if the hero made it to the end of the story alive. He always did! It was always a comforting thought.

Recently, as the Covid 19 pandemic made it's impact on all of our lives, when I would fret at the dinner table about our futures, one of my dinner companions would stop me in my tracks to say "Remember who wins in the end!" I would find myself thinking about how Jeremiah thought, as he sat in the bottom of that Jerusalem well, and it would give me some new hope and assurance.

I had the same thought when I read Timothy Keller's new book "Hope In The Times Of Fear." At its conclusion he makes these observations: "To have hope in God is not an uncertain, anxious wish that he will affirm (our) plan, but to recognize that he and he alone is trustworthy; that everything else will let you down and that his plan is infinely wise and good. If I believe in the resurrection of Jesus that confirms that there is a God who is both good and powerful, who brings light out of darkness and who is patiently working out a plan for his good, and the good of the world. Christian hope means that I stop betting my life and happiness on human agency and rest in him."

He then goes on to add: "Isaiah 40:31 says that those 'who hope in the Lord' are not anxiously holding on but always 'renewing their strength' and even 'soaring.' Hope in God leads to 'running and not growing weary' and 'walking and being faint.'"

"Real courage comes with self forgetfulness based on joy. It comes from a deep conviction that we here on earth are trapped temporarily in a little corner of darkness, but that the universe of God is an enormous place of light and high beauty and that is our certain final destiny. It is because of Jesus. He was so committed to bringing us into that light and high high beauty that lost all glory and gladness and was plunged into the depths so that we can know "that weeping may stay for the night but rejoicing comes in the morning."

Defiance comes from looking at ourselves. Hope comes from looking at him. What more needs to be said. Bring on tomorrow! Bring on all of my tomorrows!

EIGHT

Day By Day, We Live Our Lives One Day At A Time

With every passing day, the words get louder and louder. "Make the most of every day!" Sometimes, I think, I am the only one who hears them, but I am sure I am not. Due to the shortness of our longevity, make the most of every day, week or month. They will never come back!. In writing to his brother Theo, on the death of their father, Vincent Van Gogh wrote: "Life isn't long for anyone, and the question is just - do something with it."

Cliff Edwards reminds us that Van Gogh was more than a painter; his letters to his brother and others remind us of that. There was significant evidence of that. It makes one wonder how much people really know of us. Vincent was a disappointment to his father, a pastor, who never lived to see his son become famous.

Be that as it may, Van Gogh did not let the limitations his father set on him, limit his slow development, and the world is better because of his frustrated development. His poetic, creative and original mind opened up startling insights on the creative life. There was so much to be found, of spiritual significance, in his developing life. When you read his letters and then see his paintings in the light of his theological depth and understanding you should feel challenged to allow your family, friends and others, to get a glimpse of why you do what you do, and what they can learn about you through them.

I wonder how many of us live so fast that we never let our lives catch up with us: and never let it continue to be connected? Many times I found people suggesting to me and others, to keep a diary, spiritual or otherwise. How many times did I read about or quote from letters that people sent, or saved that offered wisdom to those who followed them, children and others?

Words have become cheap in the computer age. It is easy to write things down, and easier to erase them, before we take them into account. Let me remind you, with this word of caution: put some of your discoveries on paper: have them sticking out of one of your books, so they will be discovered before the book is discarded. The world might be the richer because of it.

The world has so much to learn, and you have something to share with it, Don't forget to leave your wisdom for another day to discover it.

NINE

On Hearing The Voice Of God

For most of my adult life: from High School on through College and Graduate School and all the years that followed, I read about individuals to whom God had spoken, and frankly was jealous of them. He had never said anything to me, at least so I thought. And then, several years ago, I read a book by Bill Hybels, which he entitled "Whisper," and I learned all about how God speaks, and how to listen to him and hear what he has to say. (The book, for some reason, is no longer available, so I can't refresh my memory as to what he said, I just know that I learned what I needed to know. Hybels got into some trouble at The Willow Creek Church. In any event, if you can get a copy, it is worth the read.)

I was reminded of my wonderful discovery while reading A.Z. Tozer's classic book, "The Pursuit of God." Tozer writes: "I believe that much of our religious unbelief is due to a wrong conception and a wrong feeling for the Scripture truth. A silent God suddenly began to speak in a book, and when the book was finished lapsed back into silence again, forever. Now we read the book as the record of what God said when he was, for a brief time, in a speaking mood. The facts are that God is not silent, nor has never been silent. It is the nature of God to speak . . . The Bible is the inevitable outcome of God's continuous speech."

Frankly, God is speaking to me quite a lot these days. Perhaps it is because I am retired now, and have a lot of time to listen. Possibly it is because I have a lot to learn. Maybe it is because He has a lot of things for me to do. Anyway, whatever the reason, he often talks to me at night, while I am lying in bed, even as I sleep. It is amazing how many directives I seem to receive, and when I follow them the next day, how amazing the results seem to be.

Today, enlightened by my new awareness, I now see how many things I did as a result of "feelings" I had or felt and acted on, that had an impact on my life or directly on someone close to me. Sadly, there are many things, as I look back on my life, that I did not do, and I am the poorer because of it, and so, very likely, is someone else.

I read somewhere of someone who would begin their day by reading from the Scripture until they found themselves directed to do something; would stop reading and go out and do it. God would speak to them; they would respond and then, when possible, begin reading again until they found "a new directive" which they would go out and do. I have never done that. Maybe it is worth a try? Would it be something you should try?

You, and the world you live in might be the better for it. God is speaking. Do you hear him? Let me say that again: GOD IS SPEAKING! DO YOU BEAR HIM?

TEN

Your Life May Have Only One Lesson To Share: Be Sure It's The Right One!

We are growing up a nation of liars! Let me say that again, so listen carefully. We are growing up a nation of liars! What I was severely punished for saying, while I was growing up, is now part of the character of our nations leaders.

For years we have been told that the leaders of many nations in the world cannot be counted on to do what they say they are going to do. Now our politicians, from the top of the food chain to the bottom do it every day. And they do it without any semblance of guilt.

A number of years ago, a judge in one of our Southern states was removed from office because he had a replica of the Ten Commandments placed in his building. Today, every one of our representatives in Washington, from the President, to members of The Senate and House of Representatives, from every tribe or nationality, ought to have a copy of them placed on a wall in their office. They are "Rules For Living." Not religious rules, but principles of personal character. I just read Adam Hamilton's book "Words Of Life." It is a study of Jesus and the promise of The Ten Commandments today. In a chapter which he entitled "I Swear To God" he makes this statement "You are the only sermon some people will ever hear, and the only Bible someone will read, and the only image of God some will ever see."

Later in the book, in a chapter entitled "Sticks And Stones And The Power Of Words" he adds this thought: "When our actions are done to impress others, rather than to be the person God calls us to be, our actions may be in the form of personal testimony."

Now I know that people will not change if left to their own recognisance, but we can change - if we want to. And we can let our feelings be known to others. So, the ball is in our court. We have to make a covenant with ourselves, and with our God "to change!" We can endeavor to always tell the truth, and to insist that people we know are lying change their way. By using the mail, and our phones and computers, we can hold them accountable, on a daily basis.

Our present lives depend upon our keeping that commitment. The future of our society and our world DEPEND UPON IT. Our God is depending upon us to follow his lead. I wonder if we can? OR, in our effort to be at peace with one another will we continue to turn our backs on the basic truths that hold our lives together?

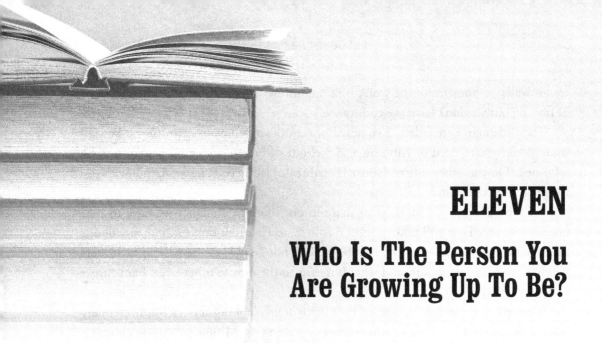

ELEVEN

Who Is The Person You Are Growing Up To Be?

In his book "Don't Give Up," Kyle Idelman offers up this thought: "There's so much freedom to he found when we get away from the obsession with what other people think or say. It feels wonderful to stop being someone else's person and to start fitting neatly into the personhood God has planned for you."

He has a few important additional thoughts later on. He says, for example, "Just keep taking one step at a time, and at the proper time you'll discover a cumulative effort. The word 'cumulative' could be defined as a gradual building up. It's not something that happens all at once but something that happens little by little. . . Each step, in the moment, may seem insignificant, but the cumulative effect of all the steps ultimately determines what race we can run." Now, we need to remember, in the long run that "we have one set of ideas about where our life is going to go, another set of actions about where it does go . . . We imagine ourselves living the kind of life we believe should be lived. But life is so daily - it's built on momentary decisions, day after day; action after action."

There is a problem in the race for everyone of us. Idelman reminds us the runners often talk about "hitting the wall" in long races. In the Boston Marathon it is called "Heartbreak Hill." He tells us the runners say to themselves "I won't survive one more step." Then he adds: "But Heartbreak Hills exist in things other than in literal running. "Hearts are broken by those hills we fail to climb. We set goals, we give our best, and we hit walls. . . Sometimes the worst isn't the hill we fail to climb; it's the experience of finding out we don't have the endurance."

Then Idelman concludes: "I've heard heaven described as oxygen for the human soul. When you're tired of running and feel out of breath, focus on heaven and be refreshed. On the other side of (your) Heartbreak Hill is your heavenly home. Keep running. Don't give up."

We have at least one message to share in our lifetime. But first we have to find out who we are. That will take most of our lives: to find that out. Only then will our message become a visible reality. Maybe we will not be able to see what it is. Others will have to tell us what it is, and what it means to them or to others. But I am sure it will be worth the wait.

We need to spend time in front of the mirror of life, looking at ourselves from many directions, and not listening to what others are telling us. Minute by minute, hour by hour, day by day we have to discover who we are and what we have to say to the world about us. Life isn't easy: it takes a long time to grow us up into the people God intends for us to be. But the journey is worth the time and the rewards will be heart warming and, maybe, earthshaking. Don't miss it.

TWELVE

How Many Of Us Are Looking For A Miracle To Happen?

When our oldest son was four years old, he was hit by a car, coming home from a birthday party. He spent about a month in the hospital suffering from his injuries. For about two weeks he bled internally. Several times each day, they emptied his urinal bag, which was filled with bloody urine.

On the second Sunday, after the accident, the minister, who was filling my pulpit, asked the congregation to pray for the boy. At approximately the same time, thirty miles away, the nurse came to empty the urinal bag. When she pulled it out from under the bed, she found its contents to be blood free: clear and very normal. Later, when we conferred with people in the church, and compared the approximate times together, it was quite evident that something, almost unbelievable had happened. We could call it nothing less than a miracle! From that moment on, when the prayers of the congregation confronted the boys needs in the hospital; recovery was on the way. Sadly, for some reason, we didn't make a point of telling anybody about it.

Recently, I was reading the introductory chapters in Eric Melaxas' book, "Miracles." This is what he had to say: "One man's miracle is another man's eye rolling. What's the big deal? Weird coincidence. . . If God is behind a miracle, and we can agree that that is what ultimately makes a miracle a miracle, then a large part of his performing the miracle, has to do with communicating with the people who are observing or experiencing the miracle. . . ". . why would God perform a miracle if no one realized he had done it? How can we ever conceive of a miracle apart from it being a communication from God to one or more people, at the very least to let them know he exists and cares for them?"

Melaxas goes on to say: "Miracles point to something beyond themselves. . . To God himself. That's the point of miracles - to point us beyond our world to another world . . . If miracles exist at all, they exist not for their own sake, but for us, to point us toward something beyond. To someone beyond."

But we learned in that hospital experience that miracles are personal, not just corporate. God satisfied a need in our lives: that was the reason for his action. Maybe we failed in not telling more people about it, but I don't think God was concerned about that. Rather, he reached in from his world to touch us in our world, and we were the benefisheries of that divine action.

SO KEEP YOUR EYES OPEN. God is at work in your world too. You don't want to miss out on what he is doing.

THIRTEEN

Don't Presume To Write The End Of Your Life's Story

I recently purchased a copy of the newest novel by the author of my oldest son's favorite author.. One of mine too. It is the story of a young basketball player, who was growing up on the African continent. He was selected to play on his national team in a tournament in the United States. The team lost out in one of the semifinals. He, however, decided to remain in the U.S. on a college scholarship.

His mother remained in Africa, along with his father, sister and two brothers. In the war torn area where he had lived, not long after he left, his father was killed, and his sister was abducted, and never heard from again. The mother and brothers found themselves in a UN Refugee Camp.

The story profiled his development as a young collegian and midway through the season, after much practice and a growing discipline, he led his team into the NCAA Tournament, where they advanced to the final, championship game, which they lost.

As the story progressed, I began to wonder how the author would end the story: his return to Africa, where he would return to his mother and brothers; remain in the U.S., for a second college year of basketball? The field was wide open.

The young man died of a drug overdose at a celebration party. Story over?

A man, a few years younger than I am, awakened his wife in the middle of the night, to tell her that he didn't feel well. I don't think he had any real previous problems. He died that night. I have thought, many times, about when, where and how I will pass on?

Thinking of it, last night, I was awakened to the title of this article. Don't presume to write the end of your life's story. It will come as a surprise. Just be ready for it when it happens.

In his writing "Billy Graham: The Man I Knew," Greg Laurie recalls being at the last Crusade, conducted by Bill Graham. Graham said to his audience: "You know Jesus said, 'Be ready, for in such a hour that you know not, the son of man comes.' In Amos, the fourth chapter, it says, 'Prepare to meet your God.' Are you prepared? Have you opened your heart to Jesus? Have you repented of your sins?" . . Then, Graham added: "This may be the last day of your life. You never know. The Bible says that today is the accepted time. Today is the day of salvation." (1)

Don't presume to write about the end of your life's story. It will come as a surprise. Just be ready for it when it happens!

FOURTEEN

Two Words That Spell "Thank You," "Forgive Me!"

Sometime ago, in one of my recent readings, I came across these words of C. S. Lewis" "Everyone thinks forgiveness is a lovely idea until they have something to forgive." Lewis followed that statement with another sentence: ". . the reality is, when you forgive someone you set a prisoner free - yourself." I wrote those two sentences down and I have been unable to get them out of my mind.

I once had a wonderful friend. He was a good bit older than I was, and a member of one of our Church boards. We played cards together; golf; we even went out to dinner together, on our wives birthday's. About eight years into my ministry in that Church, the Music Committee employed a new Minister of Music. He was a carefree kind of guy who did some rather foolish things. After one such act my friend came into my office to complain about him, and rightfully so.

Things got rather heated and, in an effort to support a staff member, I remember saying something that evidently offended my friend. He left the office, but not as a friend. He stopped talking to me; avoided me, and when his wife became ill, he went to another member on our staff and finally asked him to preside at her funeral.

I couldn't see the forest for the trees when it came to looking at the problem. The musician left our staff and was replaced by another. Sadly, our separation continued "because of him" I remember thinking to myself. Then I received another Call and left the Church. Still I did not have the necessary intelligence to see where the problem lay.

I guess it was several years before I was confronted by a bad memory. Sadly, my once great friend died prior to my awakening. I have lived with the guilt of that stupid mistake for now over forty years. Lewis' words literally stung my mind. Oh yes, I have been sorry for what I did, and have said to the wind, "I am sorry!" That, however, has not lessened my shame. Hopefully, some day we will meet and I will have the chance to tell him how sorry I am for what I said, and did not do. But until then . . .

All of this is to say, say your "I am sorries" as soon as you can. The reality is, "when you say your sorry," you set a prisoner free - yourself! Life is too long to carry your mistakes with you.

FIFTEEN
Are You Ever Too Old?

In her newest writing entitled "Dusk Night Dawn" Anne Lamott offers us these words of reflection: "I mostly love being in the third third of my life, as it is the easiest that life has ever been, except for well, the bodily aspects and the dither and the fogginess . ." "In the third third of life you may become just as miserable and prickly as ever, but you cycle through more quickly. You remember other dark nights of the soul and how by dawn they always broke. You discover that everything helps you learn who you are, and this is why we are here. You roll your eyes at yourself more gently. You sigh and go make yourself a cup of tea."

I presume, or at least I mathematicly presume that Ms Lamott is in her sisties, looking forward to her next thirty or so years. Yes, they are good years. I have lived most of them. I hope to live all of them, productively!

Louie Giglio reminds us of the call of Abraham, away back in the Old Testament book of Genesis: "Go from your country and your kindred and your father's house to the land that I will show you. (12:1) Giglio retranslates the words: "just pack up and go." The call came with a promise: "I will make of you a great nation, and I will bless you and make your name great, so that you will be a blessing . . and to you all the families of the earth shall be blessed." (v 2-3)

Giglio continues: "Notice that Abraham's promise only came on the backside of God's calling. The call was first to step forward into the unknown with God. Only then would the blessing come." The Bible specifically notes that Abraham was seventy five years old when all this went down. (v 4) This blows up two myths. First, that a person needs to have life all figured out when he or she is twenty: and the second is that God doesn't give great callings to people when they are older. God never wants anybody to check out, no matter how old they are. God is looking for people to take steps based not on age but on how we're gazing at his greatness. Up to the moment when we die, everything is fair game. God wants us to keep an open hand, continually saying, "I trust you to lead me.":

Lamott has a lot of years to live and "probably many promises to keep before she goes to sleep." And so do you! So keep on learning and doing. The world is waiting for you to do the bidding of your Heavenly Father. And if you don't follow through and do it, well - what then?

SIXTEEN
A Pattern For Coping

There is an old legend of how birds got their wings. According to that legend, the little birds didn't have wings, at first, so they would just scamper about on the ground. But one day God got worried about them. So, that night, while the birds were asleep, God attached wings to their sides.

The next morning, when the little birds woke up they felt burdened and bothered by those heavy, cumbersome things attached to their sides: they felt awkward and weighted down. It was very difficult for them to move about. Those wings were a nuisance. They complained and fussed and felt sorry for themselves. But then some of the little birds began to move their wings, and they were surprised at how graceful it felt. They exercised their wings and then suddenly some of them began to fly. Soon others also began to try it and they also found themselves flying.

Now the point of the legend is obvious, I think. It contains a beautiful lesson for life, namely this; what seemed at first to be a heavy, great burden to the little birds became their means of flight, the means by which they could soar into the skies above them.

Friends - our problems can become opportunities. Our problems can become the means by which we can soar into a higher level, a higher level of maturity and a higher level of faith. With the help of God; with God on our side, we can cope, and so we can know that we can live a triumphant life, today!

We are called to move through our problems, not around them - not away from them but through them. So it is important that we learn and know that we are not walking alone; that God is walking with us; that we come to know what he is like and what he wishes for us. Friends: that knowledge will change your life! You can count on it!

SEVENTEEN

The Growing Up Years Are So Important

He was just a college sophomore. Still very wet behind the ears. He had so much he wanted to do; to learn. He needed to accumulate some easy credit hours while digging deeply into other areas of study.

He came across a three hour course in Music Appreciation: the study of classic symphonic music. He visited the professor's office and after some initial conversation, he offered the teacher a "deal." "The professor could pick out one movement from each of ten symphonies. He would play them each once and if the young man could name eight of the movements played (from what symphony) he would receive an "A" in the course, and not have to attend any classes. The professor thought about the proposal for a few minutes, and agreed to the deal, with a smile.

The new day the young man took a chair in the office and the professor began to play the music he had selected. The student named each of the ten movements; floored the teacher with his knowledge, and the deal was consummated.

Upon being questioned as to his knowledge of the music, the sophomore shared his answer When he entered the ninth grade, his Dad had told him that he and his son were going to attend the performances of the cities Symphony, each Sunday afternoon of the orchestras musical season. So, every Sunday, at 3:00 P.M. the father and his son were in their seats for the weekly concert. The boy said he didn't really like being there: he had other things that he wanted to do, but the father was not to be denied his decision. It was a true "Father-Son Outing." I suspect that some, today, would call it "child abuse."

For five years, including his freshman year in college, when he had to drive to the city to attend the concert (a distance of some thirty miles each way) the young man and his Dad attended the concerts together, with a limited number of interruptions.

By the end of that period, the boy "loved" classical music. By the time he was in graduate school, the lad had a collection of over eight hundred (vinal) records, and it continued to grow until his death, prematurely at the age of sixty three.

I wonder how many people have interests to share, other than sports, with their offspring, with their neighbors; with a friend?. What are your interests: music, knitting, cards, coins, whatever? Have you ever thought of sharing that interest with someone else? You might be the better for it. So might someone else. Even now, in your old age.

EIGHTEEN

Encouragement Is Always Just Around The Corner

I have always written that I have lived a very blessed life, both personally and professionally. I shall continue to echo that feeling whenever I am asked. Oh, I have had those times when I have found myself in the midst of some down moments but I have always felt that was one of life's ways; sometimes up and sometimes down.

I was reminded of that when reading Eric Metaxas' book "Miracles." He reminded me that "one should not blame God for one's failures if one is greatful to him for life's successes." Rather, he adds ". . in a kind of Chestertoniam inversion, it's correct to say that we cannot truly thank God for the good things unless we also thank him for the bad things." . . . So, Metaxas suggests "if we trust the God we know . . . we know that he means well toward us at all times and in every conceivable way, so it follows that we can actually trust him with everything, including our failures and our difficulties . ." "So if he is actually the God who loves us beyond anything we can imagine, even the bad things can ultimately be a blessing. In fact, God wants us to know that, because our sufferings will be easier to bear if we know God is with us in the midst of them, leading us toward something ultimately redemptive and beautiful."

This is where God gave me a new word of encouragement. Metaxas writes, "So those who have faith in the God of the Bible can know that even if we don't get the miracle we are praying for, we can relax and trust that God is nonetheless leading us toward something through whatever it is we are enduring."

It makes me wonder: is life, among other things, a "waiting game?" That is, I have to wait until tomorrow to see how today will work itself into the whole process, and only then will I be able to see how it will work itself out in the grand scheme of things.

Life has to be lived out one day at a time; I can't rush it, no matter how I try. What is the statement believed and shared by so many; "I don't know what tomorrow may bring, but I know who holds tomorrow in his hands."

I have had many of my prayers answered. However, I have been praying a prayer, now, for almost twenty years, that has still not been answered, at least in the way I want it to be answered. I know there is an answer out there. I just need to "wait" until God is ready to share it with me, or I am ready to hear it.

"Waiting!" I hope and "pray" that I will have the patience to wait until the answer comes. Maybe today? Maybe tomorrow? Only God knows! And I am not God, no matter what I sometimes think.

How good are you at "waiting?" Maybe better than you think you are. As you look back on the events that transpired in your life, how has your prayer life effected them? You might be very surprised by your discoveries.

NINETEEN

Becoming Who You Are Supposed To Be!

I can still remember the day I made my career choice. Where I was, and even the individual who sent me on my way. I never deviated from that decision and it was consistent with the time in which I lived, Individuals, then, usually began and ended their lives in the same career.

My grandfather was a carpenter/cabinet maker. He did that job, very successfully, all of his life. Late, in his working life, he fell off a roof and was forced, by my Dad, to complete his working years, laboring in a factory (Allis Chalmers.) But, he still worked with his hands and accomplished some amazing results. My Dad was an educator all of his life, though he could have been a carpenter, because he also was very competent with his hands and did some major work in our home and in his retirement home in his later years. But they were one career people I developed none of those significant skills. I probably would have gone hungry if left to the work of my hands.

Times have surely changed. Each of our three children has changed the direction of their lives a number of times.

I was reminded of these limitations when I came across these words of David Jeremiah. He quoted them in one of his books "Count It All Joy,":

"Be who you is,
because if you who is you ain't.
you ain't who you is"

It was Steven Covey who wrote: " . . seeing the goal clearly before you set out to reach it is the difference between those who achieve their objectives and those who do not." I am sure that is true when you have defined a goal, - but we can have several goals.

Who was I intended to be? I probably won't ever know. The days of my decision making are long gone. But I still wonder. Maybe you do too? Let me suggest that if it is not too late in your life, that you do some investigation. Go back in your imagination, to the day when you made your initial decision, or to a subsequent time when you moved from one career to another and begin there? Did you make the right move then? If not, in what direction do you need to move now, to correct that decision? Maybe it is not too late. Just follow Mr. Covey's suggestion.

In his autobiography, "Heart Of Steal" Bill Cowher concludes: "God never said "Here's your life. You get a contract. It's loaded with everything you want." No, it doesn't work like that. You can't take the years you think you are going to are going to get and chart them out. You take what you're given and try to fashion the best life you can get out of it."

I guess I made the right decision back then, but now, at an advanced age, I am beginning to move in another direction. I am beginning to put words on paper - to write! Maybe something will come of it? Who knows? It's worth a try.

What about you?

TWENTY

Some Issues Are Worth The Argument

We live on the campus of a Senior Living facility. Needless to say, it is a confining experience. Every evening we eat together in a restaurant on campus. The day I began reading the book "Uncommon Ground." by Tim Keller, one of the residents died.. They had a "Celebration of Life" service, a week or so later. The family said "No Religious Talk!" please. I didn't go. And as I looked around our dining room, the next day, I thought to myself, "many of these people are not ready to die, and they don't know it." The Jewish folk often gather for worship on Friday evenings and many others attend worship during the week or on Saturday or Sunday. But the others?

One of my friends remarked to me about my concern. "Well, we have a forgiving God! In his writing, Mr Keller wrote: "We can be humble because, as members of God's family, we know we are entirely dependent on the grace of God extended to us in Christ, which we use to love others. We can tolerate those with whom we profoundly disagree because the love we have in Christ does not insist on its own way, but rather hears and endures as it waits on the day we will see all things clearly and fully."

A chapter later, Keller quotes the words of Jesus, in the Gospel of Mark, "Anyone who wishes to be a follower of mine must leave self behind, take up his cross and come with me. What does a man gain by winning the whole world at the cost of his true self?" Then he adds, "You can only become yourself if you do what you were created to be - to serve and obey God unconditionally, to love and rejoice in him above all things. There could not be a more cultural thing." And all God's people said. "Amen!"

Keller went on to speak about Jesus' reminding us that meat needs salt the way a culture needs the influence of the individual Christian disciple: "Just as salt can only help the meat if it retains its saltiness." Jesus added, "Then we can only help the world if we retain our integrity." That is, if salt has exactly the same chemical composition as the meat, it cannot help the meat. And if Christians become like everyone else, in their society, they can't help that society. We can only help and benefit our society if we are different from it; if we maintain a Christian identity rather than adopt a secular one."

Then Keller concludes his remarks with this thought: "The Gospel removes fear. While we should be concerned to not needlessly offend people, the assurance of God's love and his acceptance should give us the courage to face criticism and disappointment."

Yes! Like the rich young ruler, we have some real thinking to do, and some significant responsibilities to carry out.

TWENTY ONE
Making A New Path To Walk On

The writers gathered together to write the book "Uncommon Ground" were asked to respond to the question about ",, being a follower of Jesus Christ in these days." Writing from the vantage point of being an entrepreneur, Rudy Carrasco told his reader's of a three step program that he used to give strength to his actions. The second step in that program was "You make the road as you walk."

Reflecting on those words, Carrasco noted: "The realization that there may be no path, no role model, and no precedent for the course of action one must take can be demoralizing. . . But the council to 'make the road as you walk' only tells me that there is a path, however costly, that lies ahead."

Walker Percy offers these words of hope "What is the nature of the search you ask, Really it is very simple, at least for the fellow like me, so simple that it is easily overlooked. The search is what anyone would undertake if he were not sunk in the everydayness of his own life. This morning, for example, I felt as if I had come to my self on a strange island. And what does such a castaway do? Why he pokes around the neighborhood and he doesn't miss a trick. To become aware of the possibility of the search is to do something. Not to be on to something is to be in despair." The suggestion is that we need to be constantly on the lookout for things that God might have us do.

Dr. Anthony Bradley provides an illuminating perspective on the nature of (this) salt in a fertilizer. In a 2016 Christianity Today article, he cites the work, of several agriculturists, who noted that the ancient world understood salt as fertilizer. . . . and continues (is) that Christians are called to go where nothing is growing right now and help bring new life. . . The followers of Jesus Christ are sent on a mission to stimulate growth in the parts of the world that are barren, and to be mixed into the manure piles of the world so that God can use that fertilizer to bring new, virtuous life." Corrasco then adds, "I see more clearly now that when Christians respond in faith and choose to be entrepreneurial, we are fertilizing the world and bringing life to places that need it."

Carasso concludes with this challenge: We need to be interested in creating something out of nothing. It means "moving in that direction despite (y)our fears and anxieties. We may at times be less than hopeful, . . . but we should remember that we can creatively address challenges in our communities because the God we serve is creative. He has made us in his image and has given us the capacity to rise to whatever work he gives us to do."

Nothing is said about completing the job we start: only starting it, believing that God will complete whatever he urges us to start.

You are on your mission field right now, no matter your age or whereabouts. So why not be about your father's business - starting right now! Pray now: Find the path God wants you to travel.

TWENTY TWO
Endless Possibilities

In his writing on "The Epistle To The Philippians." "Count It All Joy," David Jeremiah shares this wonderful illustration filled with optimism and hope,

"In one of the many attempts to scale Mt. Everest, before the successful climb in 1953, a team of mountain climbers made a final dash for the summit.. Their courageous attempt failed and today they lie buried in the eternal snow. One of the party who had stayed below, when the final assault was attempted, returned to London. One day, as he was giving a lecture on mountain climbing, he stood before a magnificent picture of Mt. Everest. As he concluded his lecture, he turned around and addressing the mountain said: 'We have tried to conquer you and failed: we tried again and you beat us; but we shall beat you, for you cannot grow bigger but we can.'"

What more does one have to say, as we face the many problems that life throws at us? Even if you do not have a god, you can call upon, it offers you the possibilities of trying again and again and again, as you keep growing. And if you are not walking alone, but walking with the Son of God, Jesus Christ, at your side, the flood lights of assurance are ready to open and give you the victory.

As Jeremiah went on to say: "Just as the mountain climber can never give up, so long as there is an unconquered peak, so The Apostle Paul could not let the Philippian believers give up until they reached maturity. His challenge to them was to keep on walking, keep on growing, keep on climbing until they reached their potential in Christ."

". . the one thing I do, however, is to forget what is behind me and do my best to reach what is ahead. So I run straight toward the goal in order to win the prize, which is God's call through Christ Jesus to the life above." Philippians 3:13b-14

It's a wonderful way to live out your life: - with endless possibilities waiting ahead of you. God bless!

TWENTY THREE
Hidden Truths/ Valuable Assets

Sometime ago I began to discover some almost bidden truths and valuable assets to be found in the writings of many people. I suspect that they knew they were there, maybe not; but in any event I came upon them and they gave me a great deal to think about. It was like "panning for gold" in the California mountains.

I came across one of them in a contribution made by Sarah Groves, a singer and song writer in the book "Uncommon Ground." She quotes one of her producers, Charlie Peacock, as saying; "Here's what I have figured out for myself: 'My life is going to tell a story whether I try or not.. It's going to tell a story that says, here is what a follower of Jesus is, that is what he or she is interested in, that is what he or she believes and trusts, this is what he or she thinks is important.'

Isn't that what our lives are to be all about: about walking with Jesus?

Eugene Petersen, the author/Bible translator is said to have said: "I like people who act like they know where they are going. I like people who live aggressively - who have a purpose. I want to be that kind of person."

Well, what is the plan for your life that you are now living under? You don't have one? Shouldn't you have one? Why not stop now and think about it? Maybe write something out, revise it tomorrow or next week and begin living like you know where you are going. Maybe you will unearth some new, hidden truth, and it will become a valuable asset.

"Now great crowds accompanied him" and he turned and said to them. "If anyone comes to me and does not hate his own father and mother and wife and children and brothers and sisters, and yes, and even his own life, he cannot be my disciple. Whoever does not bear his own cross and come after me cannot be my disciple. For which of you desiring to build a tower, does not sit down and count the cost, whether he has enough to complete it? Otherwise, when he has laid the foundation and is not able to finish, all who see it began to mock him, saying "This man began to build and was not able to finish." Or what King going out to encounter another king in war will not sit down first and deliberate whether he is able with ten thousand to meet him who comes against him with twenty thousand? And if not, while the other is yet a great way off, he sends a delegation and asks for terms of peace. So therefore, any one of you who does not renounce all that he has cannot be my disciple." Luke 14:25-33.

So, now, let me ask you, again, the same question, "Under what plan are you living?" Think about it. And once you have, do something about it; maybe do some planning?

TWENTY FOUR
The Proof Is In The Pudding

Some years ago, as the church was facing one of its' many challenges, then Archbishop of Canterbury Rowan Williams made this observation: "The Church is not ours to save." Commenting further on that same thought, a Canadian rector added: "We are called only to be good stewards of what we have been given. God will do what God will do."

In his introduction to a book, written by Erwin Lutzer, "We Will Not Be Silenced," Dr. David Jeremiah quoted these words of Lutzer: "I want to inspire us to have the courage to walk toward the fire and not run away from the flame. God has brought us to this cultural moment, and our future cannot be taken for granted. As has been said 'In a time of universal deception, telling the truth is a revolutionary act.'"

Lutzer writes: "Yet today there are calls for evangelicals to make Christianity into a more inclusive religion. There are widespread efforts to make the narrow door wider and even to affirm the salvation of well meaning people of other religions. So called progressive Christians advance their causes under the banner of love and compassion. In the process, the hard truths of Christianity are either redefined or ignored."

It was Peter the Apostle who said and wrote: ". . be ready at all times to answer anyone who asks you to explain the hope you have in you, but do it with gentleness and respect." (1 Peter 3:15b)

Years ago, I read a book by the late Senator William Fulbright entitled "The Arrogance of Power." In it, as I remember he said that if we Americans actually practiced the things we profess, every country in the world would want to be like us. Apply that to the faith we profess to practice and we would be overcome by the number of people who would want to profess that same faith.

We are called to know what we believe and what it means to us and to proclaim and practice that faith, no matter what.

Lutzer writes;: "What a special privilege it is to represent Christ at this pivotal moment in history. We are called for such a time as this. And we must pray that our light might shine more brightly than ever in our darkening world."

Do your best, and remember "God will do what God will do!" Amen?

TWENTY FIVE

Keep The Shoe On The Right Foot

I've spent a lot of time in Dothan! I've invited a good many people to join me there. The reason was and is that the episode speaks of Elisha and his battle with the King of Syria in that place. It reminds us that God is always where we are when we face the many battles that life throws at us.

Most of you know the story. The armies of the Syrian King had tracked the prophet Elisha to Dothan. They had surrounded the place where Elisha was staying. When his servant got up in the morning and looked outside, he saw the army and knew they were in deep trouble. When he apprised the prophet of their situation the prophet rolled over and went back to sleep. When the servant pressed him with their problem, Elisha said to the servant, "Don't worry! We have more on our side than they have on their's." He then said to the Lord: "O Lord, open his eyes that he may see." - and immediately the servant saw, behind the King's men, "a hillside covered with horses and chariots of fire all around them." I was reminded of the hymn, "Open Our Eye's, And Let Us See, glimpses of truth, you have for us." My message to anyone and everyone in trouble - "Just open your eyes, God has your back."

Lately, however, I find myself in that servant's shoes. All I seem to see is the problems that surround me. I need an Elisha to tell me of God's presence in my life and situations. I need to be reminded that God has my back, protected! No one is reminding me and I am living as a beaten man. For some reason I can't open my eyes. I need someone to encourage me to get them open.

There are people out there who need an Elisha in their lives. Could you be that person for someone? If nothing else, you could tell them the story in II Kings, chapter 6. Invite them to go to Dothan with you. I know I need someone to remind me of the story on a daily basis, with enthusiasm. Could you be that person in someone's life?

"O Lord, open their eyes and let them SEE!"

TWENTY SIX

We Were Built To Follow The Owner's Manual

Like many priests and ministers, and most rabbi's, I was paid to read. I spent many hours during the day and many night time hours gathering information to share in teachable moments with the people who paid me to do it. Then, following my retirement, I began to share that information with others on the printed page.

Then, for some reason, some months ago, I lost my desire to read. I could not muster up the ambition to pick up a book and read it. They lay on a shelf, next to my reading chair, unopened. I started moving in the direction of the land of depression. I became despondent and anxious. I started to lose control of my life.

Then, one morning, while my wife was shopping in a nearby grocery store, I spent some time, maybe the better word is, "I determined to waste some time in a bookstore." It's name shall go by "unlisted." I picked up a book by Tim Keller which he had entitled "Every Good Endeavor." I found a chair and began to read it.

Several pages into it I came across these words: "(So) the commandments of God in the Bible are a means of liberation because through them God calls us to be what he built us to be. Cars work when you follow the owner's manual and honor the design of the car. If you fail to change the oil, no one will fine you or take you to jail, your car will simply break down because you violated its nature. You suffer a natural consequence. In the same way human life works properly only when it is conducted in line with the owner's manual;" the commandments of God. If you disobey the commands, not only do you grieve and dishonor God, you are actually acting against your own nature as God has designed you.

When God speaks to disobedient Israel, as he did in Isaiah 68 he says: "I am the Lord your God, who teaches you what is best for you, who directs you in the way you should go. If you had paid attention to my commands, your peace would have been like a river, your well being like the waves of the sea.." (Isaiah 48:17-18)

Then he adds: "And so it is with work which (in rhythm with the rest) is one of the Ten Commandments: "Six days you shall labor and do all your work." (Exodus 20:9) In the beginning God created us to work and now he calls us and directs us unambiguously to live out that part of our design. This is not a burdensome command, it is an invitation to freedom."

We were created to work as long as God expects us to work and maybe, if we stop too soon, he is determined not to let us stop. Hence my situation at that particular time in my life. I bought several interesting books and, once again, began to read.

Have you stopped doing what God created you to do, - too soon? How much is there in life for you to still do? Maybe it is time to do some investigating. Put this book down and get to it!!

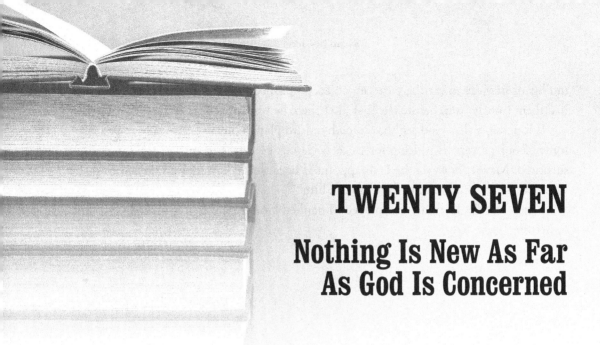

TWENTY SEVEN

Nothing Is New As Far As God Is Concerned

I think he knew from before the beginning. From before the very beginning: from before what we know as "The Fall!" As he began to make his initial plans: when the "Thus Saith The Lord Words" had not yet been spoken, he knew. "Man was not going to hold his own against the wiles of The Satan.. Eve was going to succumb to his temptations,,, and then Adam. He knew it was going to happen. Maybe he talked it over with "The Son" He saw it all being played out before him. He knew what was going to happen before he spoke those initial words of creation.

And he knew what we were going to do before we did it. There have been no surprises in life as far as God is concerned: we are the only one's being surprised. In his book "How To Pray" C. S. Lewis notes: ". . when God, at the moment of creation fed the first event into the framework of "the laws" - first set the ball rolling - he determined the whole of history of nature.

Foreseeing every part of that history, he intended every part of it. If he had wished (for something else) he would have made the first event slightly different.:

I had a Seminary Professor, a student of Lewis', who told us he believed that God could answer all of our prayers, and not have to change any of his plans. I guess we could call it "contingency planning."

I read somewhere that if you wanted to read through the Bible, you should start in four places: in Genesis 1: in Ezra, in Matthew, and in Acts. It was as if God took four mulligans in order to get the creation job accomplished; to get it done right . . and he had them in play from before the first "Let there he was spoken . ."

Is it possible that God still has some hands to play in our lives: is ready to answer some of our prayers; is waiting for us to voice our concerns in prayer? God is never surprised. Maybe, however, he is disappointed because we have not awakened to our situation. What is he waiting for us to ask him?

When was the last time you prayed? Thanked God for a blessing? Asked God for something?

TWENTY EIGHT

"We Are Having A Hard Time Finding Out The Truth"

I was reading Tim Keller's book "Every Good Endeavor," with the television set centered on one of the news channels. Keller's writing was speaking of God's words to Adam and Eve, following their capitulation to the Evil One in Genesis, chapter 3. God was speaking of the punishment that would come their way: "You will have to work hard all of your life to make it produce enough food for you. It will produce weeds and thorns." (3:17b-18) According to Keller "the weeds and thorns" had to do, not only with produce but also with the problems that life would bring to them.

As those words walked before my mind the news anchor was speaking of the falsehoods that politicians, of both major political parties keep telling us. It dawned upon me that in our day and age we will not know the truth because our politicians are, to often, incapable of telling us the truth. They seek to overwhelm us with their political diatribe, as they seek to gain more and more power over us.

We continue to be in the midst of the Caronavirus pandemic and in their endeavor to hold us at bay, and as a result of their hate for one another, and their disregard for us, they continue to lie. What was it that Jesus said: "And you shall know the truth and the truth will set you free." (John 8:32) Well they don't tell us the truth and, as a result, they seek to control our every move and all of our actions.

I guess we could stop paying attention to our television screens; at least those that broadcast the news. However, then what would we know about anything? We need to know what's going on: what is really going on? And I do not know where to find the truth?

What is it? Where is it? Is it just possible that this is something we need to ask God about? How will he get the answer to us? Wow! That is something we need to think about: pray about and then listen for an answer.

TWENTY NINE

Were You Made For A Particular Moment?

During these Pandemic years, in which I have been living, I have been reading about the historical moments recorded in the Old Testament book of Esther. Max Lucado notes that he can remember two movies that captured the story. I don't remember either of them.

You will, perhaps, remember the story. The King of Persia had some problems with his Queen. He had her removed from the Palace. A Jew, by the name of Mordecai saw a way of getting his niece placed in a contest to become the new Queen. He was successful. No one, however, knew she was a Hebrew.

The King's Prime Minister was possessed by a hate for the Jewish people in the Kingdom. He plotted to have them exterminated. Mordecai learned of the plot and realized that only Queen Esther could stop it; but it could mean that she could lose her life in the process. Naturally, she was reluctant to put her life on the line. However, Mordecai knew she was the only one who could successfully deal with the problem. Acknowledging all of her assets, he challenged her with these words: "Who knows but that you have come to your position for such a time as this." Wow!

As the story unfolds, Esther came to her senses, went to the King, and put flesh on Mordecai's plan. In the end she wins; the Prune Minister is put to death and the Hebrews live another day or days, or many days.

In Lucado's words: "Each of our lives intersects with opportunities in which we can come alongside the work of God. We won't speak to a Persian King. Very few will lead a movement of liberty. But heaven will offer each one of us, without exception, the privilege of participating in Holy Work." The community where we live? Your city, state or nation? We may be in the big leagues; In the midst of a family situation?

The question that is before us in each of our Pandemic Moments is, "When the moment comes for us, will we be ready?

I do know when that will be? Maybe it has already come and is past, for you. Maybe God had to raise up someone else to get his work accomplished? Makes you wonder, doesn't it?

What are your particular gifts? What benefits have you received so that you will be ready when the opportunity comes, or comes again? Maybe it is time to take an inventory.

I wonder; think about it now - Is your time still out there?

THIRTY

Believe it: God has your back!

I will still reading Max Lucado's writing "You Were Made For This Moment." Esther, the queen, was contemplating Mordicai's challenge: "Who knows but that you have come to your royal position for such a time as this?" Would she go before the King, at the risk of her own life, or not? She made her decision, though she had a proviso or two.

We read in the book of Esther: "Esther sent Mordecai this reply: Go and get all the Jews in Susa together; hold a fast and pray for me. Don't eat or drink anything for three days and nights. My servant girls and I will be doing the same. After that I will go to the king, even though it is against the law. If I must die for doing it, I will die." Mordecai then left and did everything that Esther had told him to do,"

"On the third day of her fast Esther put on her royal robes and went and stood in the inner courtyard of the palace facing the throne room . . . When the king saw Queen Esther standing outside, she won his heart, and he held out to her the golden sceptre."

Do you get if? Lucado did! Speaking for himself and, also, for Queen Esther, he wrote: "Don't think for a moment that you have what it takes . . Yet don't think for a second that God won't give you what you need."

God had her back! That was what she had been taught on Mordecai's knee. This is what she believed; so she marched into the courtyard of the palace, unafraid – and God carried the day!

So it was with Jesus in the Garden of Gethsemane. Left alone by his disciples he prayed: "'Father,' he said. "If you are willing, remove this cup of suffering away from me. Yet, not my will but yours be done." "An angel from heaven appeared to him and strengthened him." (Luke 22:42-43) He knew God had his back, and he was ready to go!

I think these two incidents ask the faith question. "Do you believe that God has your back?" If you do, whatever life throws at you, you know you can handle it. . If you don't believe that, take time to think it through. Where is God as far as your life is concerned?

Do you believe that God has your back? Really?

THIRTY ONE
Focus On Today

I was reading a book by Peter Davis entitled, "Dedicated." It's a great read! Davis likens our lives to a walk down a corridor that is bordered on each side by doors that are there to represent the opportunities that life offers each one of us. The book, so Davis writes, is a "case for commitment in an age of infinite browsing." As he writes: "Commitment is the first step in changing they world - and our fears of it are standing in the way of our jumping in." He then adds: "But we need not be afraid, for we have in our power the ability to perform the slow but necessary work of turning visions into projects, values into practices and strangers into neighbors. But only if we commit."

But commitment demands planning and planning demands having goals. So a successful, fulfilling life requires having an idea about where we are going and knowing where we are going demands that we have a plan or a goal in mind.

As we begin our journey down the corridor that we will call "our life," we have to have some idea of where we want to go: about our life's goals. As we face one opportunity alter another, that life throws in our direction, we need to balance it out with our planned goal. We will, of course, in our life's development open many doors, and close many of them, as we continue moving on.

I was reminded of some words of Jim Marshall. Marshall was a defensive lineman, who played for the Minnesota Vikings NFL Football Team (1961 to 1979). Marshall said of himself and his defensive teammates. "Our job is to meet at the Quarterback." They did this so successfully that he and those who played along with him, were given the title "The Purple People Eaters." They had a goal and they spent their professional lives reaching for it.

It requires that I ask you, "What is/are the goals toward which you are seeking to move your life today? And tomorrow, I will pose a similar question: "What are the goals toward which you are living your life today?" Before you open another door or walk any further along your life's way; think about answering the question: "What are the primary goals of my life TODAY?" if you don't know the answer to that question, you better "pause" where you are, in your life, because you may be moving in the wrong direction.

THIRTY TWO
A Successful Decision Making Process

Life has a beginning and an ending. We call the beginning "birth" and the ending "death." In the middle (this is the substance of the hiffin on our tombstone) we have an almost endless number of decisions that we must make to determine what our life will be all about..

I recently came across a book by Andy Stanley (the son of Dr. Charles Stanley) entitled "Ask It?" The under title read:: "The Question That Will Revolutionize How You Make Your Decisions." It was a great read! After I read it, I sent a copy to each of my grand kids.

The question that he poses we ask is this, on the basis of where we are, and knowing where we want go with our lives - "Is the decision we have made a wise one?" We will bring many questions to the table but, I think, Stanley would suggest that his question might be the final one.

Many writer's tell us that our lives follow the direction of our thoughts. The Apostle Paul tells us that our thoughts shape our lives"

Craig Groeschel recently wrote a book that focuses our attention on the battle in front of us: "Winning The War In Your Mind." As he notes, "In ten years we will each look in the mirror and someone will look back. That person will be shaped by the thoughts of today .The life we have is a reflection of what we think."

He then asks the question, "Do I like the direction my thoughts are taking me? And if you don't, then maybe it's time you change the way you are thinking. As any

Christian evangelist would tell you, "Decide to change your mind so God can change your life.."

No matter what you believe, to make it very personal, - if you are not happy with the way you are living, some changes will have to be made, if you do not want to end up looking at a person in the mirror that does not appeal to you.

Again, - no matter what you believe, maybe Stanley's question will be the first question you put in your question quiver. It may be the only one for a while, but it is a good one. Being a Christian, I cannot give you additional counsel, I can only get you started, and pray you find the direction you might want to go.

Is this a question that you need to regularly ask yourself?

THIRTY THREE
Important Places In Your Life

During the course of my life I had what I thought were several odd aspirations. The first was to have a front porch on which I could sit and watch the world go by. The second was to have a Patio or Deck in the backyard where I could not only read, but also think about the things of life.

I enjoyed the first aspiration in our very first Presbyterian Manse (what Presbyterians called the Home in which their preacher lived). It was in a small Western Pennsylvania County Seat town. I found my second hope fulfilled in our final home, in central Ohio. Now, in the Retirement Community, in which we live. I have found both.

I was reminded of those aspiration as I read Lee Strobel's book, "The Case For Heaven." In an interview he records with Scott McKnight, McKnight writes, When I use my imagination, I picture our homes as having a veranda for fellowship and a garden for retreat." "A Veranda?" It's a sign of hospitality." . . "before World War II, homes were built with veranda's, where people would sit in the evening with their family to greet passersby and invite them to stop and chat. But veranda's tended to disappear after the war. They were replaced by gardens in the back of the property, where people would retreat from the rest of the world."

McKnight went on to say: ". . after dinner we'd go out in the front yard to cool off and neighbors would come up and chat and hang out. It was great! I believe heaven will strike the perfect balance of privacy and devoted love of God, as well as fellowship and devoted love of family and friends."

"Heaven will be a fellowship of differents - everyone reconciled and forgiven, all relationships characterized by trust and joy and everyone with a story to tell, one that all of us will want to hear."

It leads me to think that we can experience a heavenly experience on our porch or in our garden or patio, right now; today.

Strobel concludes, in a way better than I can: "Yes, you can know right now, with certainty -that you will revel in the goodness of God, in heaven, forever. If you believe the Jesus story as best you can, then receive his gilt of forgiveness and eternal life in a sincere prayer of repentance and faith, and you will become his child for eternity. You will dwell with God and he will dwell with you - in the new heaven and the new earth."

Like Strobel, you will find me sitting on my patio. You are welcome to come over for some conversation.

THIRTY FOUR

The Important Message of One Simple Word

In his writing "Winning The War In Your Mind," Craig Groeschel devotes an entire chapter to the word "ruminate" which he says is another translation of the word "meditate." He points our attention to Joshua 1:8, Psalm, 1:2 and at least six other passages where he tells us God directs us "to ruminate." What does ruminate mean? "Rumination is what cows do with their cud."

"Cows get a mouth full of grass, chew it up, swallow it, throw it back up in their mouths, chew it some more, swallow it again, throw it back up into their mouths again, chew it some more, swallow it again, throw it back up again, chew it some more, and swallow it again. They do this over and over.. This is what it means to ruminate."

I had written a commentary to these words by Mr. Groeschel and went to bed. As I lay there the "light bulb" went on. I had been reading my way through the Psalms, in "The Amplified Bible." There is a word used in a number of the Psalms, in 39 of them to be exact, and in one of the prophets, as well. The word is "Selah." I never really knew what it meant, and in doing some research on it, discovered that nobody else really knew or knows what it meant or means either.

However, in The Amplified Bible; it's translators chose these words "(Pause and think of that.)" (See Psalm 24:6). It sure sounds as if the writer were saying, "chew it, swallow it, throw it back up into your mouth . ." Mr. Groeschel asks the rhetorical question, How do you confront the lies of The Satan? He answers himself, "The answer is repetition of a truth. You are going to write it, think it, and confess it until you believe it." You ruminate it! You meditate on it! You take the time to seriously think about it.

I remember the story of the preacher who offered up a sermon one Sunday morning. The next Sunday he preached the same sermon. Some of his members talked about it, to themselves. The next Sunday he preached the sermon, again. Some of his members talked to each other about it. The next Sunday he preached it again. After the worship hour some members sought him out to ask him what was going on? He replied: "I am going to preach the same sermon next Sunday morning, and on every Sunday morning after that until you listen to it and follow its Biblical directives"

I wonder? How many times would your preacher, priest or rabbi have to offer up the same message week after week until you considered his/her message and responded, personally, to it?

Think about rumination. Maybe you need to put the word "Selah" at the end of every day: at the conclusion of everything you read (or think about.) It kind of plays into Andy Stanley's question, "Is it the wise thing to do?"

So, slow down. Pause!! Do some slow thinking. You might be in for a host of surprises.

THIRTY FIVE

Second Place Can Still Be A Good Place To Be!

I recently came across a book written by a then younger Southern Baptist minister by the name of Andy Stanley. It was entitled "Next Generation Leader." As its title announced, it was a book about Leadership.

Early on, Stanley quotes from a writing by Steven Covey, "The Seven Habits Of Highly Effective People." Covey wrote: "We accomplish all we do through delegation - either to time or to other people. Transferring responsibility to other skilled and trained people enables you to give your energies to other high leveraged activities. Delegation means growth, both for individuals and organizations.

Stanley, of course, was writing of positions from the top down. But, as an older man I began to look to look at the word's from the bottom up. There are many older people who have completed their run in life, but who have talents still to be used. The are retired, looking for ways of being useful. They are ready and able to provide "possibilities" to many younger leaders, in places they lack the ability to shine.

I am reminded of an older Pediatrion who served as a Medical Officer at one of our Service Academies. Then he taught at two of our major Medical Schools, before enjoying a private practice. He was a great diagnostician. One day he became legally blind, though he still could see. He had to give up his medical practice because he lost his mal-practice insurance. He spent the last years of his life serving as a volunteer in a local hospital; delivering mail and newspapers. He would have been an invaluable assistant to any other pediatrician, even to a Hospital in a sheltered advisory position, but his abilities were lost.

He probably did not shop his abilities around. The younger doctors were intimated by his age and experience. He certainly didn't need the money. All someone needed to do was to cultivate his possibilities.

On the other hand, I knew a woman who was a great Elementary teacher who, on her retirement, volunteered in one of our local schools, and continued to use her abilities.

How many of us have gifts to share with the communities around us? What more have we still to accomplish as life moves us on?

THIRTY SIX

Remember: And Never Forget The Ground Rules

A recent issue of Christian Century Magazine announced to part of the world, including me, the death of Episcopal Bishop John Shelby Spong. I have read most of Spong's books, but have never felt able to believe much of what he put on paper.. Included in the article was a reference to something that he wrote: "The world the Christian Church was born in is not the world we live in, and if you confine it to the world it was born in, Christianity will die, because that world is dying."

Spong would have had us write down a new set of Christian beliefs that are acceptable to the twenty first century, with no particular concern for what the Church has believed in and set forth in its first two thousand plus years. That is just not acceptable as far as I am concerned. First truths never change; never mind how the world has changed.

I was again reminded, as I have written earlier, of how I was taught to look at the Biblical truths that were presented to me, in the initial years of my Seminary training. What did they mean at the time they were first taught in the days of the New Testament? Second: What do they mean today? And finally, What do they mean to me? The primary truth must first be "What did they mean when they were first taught?" If the Church dies because that is what it teaches, then it deserves to die, and God will just have to start out all over again. I guess we could call that Act I. That is not going to happen, believe me.

Preachers today, at least the ones we read about, are more concerned for the "size" of their listening audience than they are about what they are teaching them. The "Give To Get" Gospel is what we seem to hear about, and that is not what the New Testament is all about. I am convicted that "size" is causing the death of the Church. When it ceases to be a "Family of Faith," and just a preaching station, the disciples suffer and one church building after another has to close its doors. Isn't that what Romans 12 is all about?

We need to hear again and again the words of the New Testament; the proclamations of the Carpenter from Nazareth: we need to know what we believe; what we really believe, and then move on into our tomorrows. Are you ready for that journey? Really ready?

Go ahead now. Say what you believe out loud! The world is listening. Say it out loud! And if you don't know what you believe, then search through that stuff that is floating around out there and finally find out.

Then, get out there and tell the world what you believe. It is waiting to hear from you. Go ahead now! Shout it out! Out bond? . . . . . . Louder!

THIRTY SEVEN

A Sentence Worth Remembering

In his writing "The Case For Heaven," Lee Strobel writes one sentence that I cannot seem to forget. It is a great read. Strobel shares an interview he had with evangelist Luis Palau. The evangelist was speaking about the reason for wanting to get into heaven.

"In my early years" Palau said, "I tended to be harsh. And that is not always a bad thing. Fear is the beginning of wisdom, and sometimes you need to put the fear of God into people, so my main theme was 'turn or burn. But" he continued. 'There's a difference between wanting to avoid hell and genuinely wanting to spend eternity with God." He went on to say: "I've (begun to emphasize) God's kindness, his generosity, his forbearance, his love, his goodness. He sets us free! What's better than that?"

Strobel countered: "And what about people who aren't Christians? What is your message to them?" Palau responded: "I'd tell them, "Don't be stupid!"" It's not something you could say from behind a pulpit: it would turn your listener's off. I would not say it, and I don't think Palau ever did either. But he could write out what he truly believed, and I would too. But it is a sentence worth remembering. One you could use in appropriate places.

"Don't be stupid!" "Don't pass up what God is offering out of his love and grace. Why embrace evil when goodness beckons? Why turn your back on heaven and choose hell? Why expose yourself to the harmful side effects of a sinful life when you can follow God's path of righteousness and healing? Don't miss the party God has waiting for you in heaven!"

I think that is a wonderful sentence, full of meaning. "Seek God. Trust him. Follow him." Hear the words of Luis Palau.: "Don't be stupid!"

THIRTY EIGHT

You Get What You Are Looking For!

Again, a thought from Craig Groeschel. "There is it story about a young man who was at a crisis point about his future and didn't know what direction to turn. His mom told him to visit a retired pastor who for many years had lived just a few houses away. Barely knowing the man but desperate for help he agreed. As the discussion finally turned toward faith, the young man said: "The problem I have is I just can't see God in this world." The elder pastor responded, quietly yet confidently. "Well, son, I have a very different problem. When I look at the same world, I cannot not see him!" Groeschel's observation was, "You find what you are looking!"

I must admit, I hear what that pastor said, and I agree with him. But there are many, many people living in our world who find themselves in the position of that young man. And what about that observation, - "You find what you are looking for?"

I heard a preacher say that a very successful investor was asked "How do you become successful?" He responded, "You find a successful person, and you follow her or him." Probably a good idea IF you want to become a successful investor or a professional in almost any field of endeavor. But how do you become a successful man or woman in the truest sense of the word?

There might be some quiet types out there but the modern media (radio, TV, newspapers and magazines) have cleared the field. I guess you could read all there is to know about Abe Lincoln and use him as your shinning example; maybe not.

So, unless you move toward the mind set of that pastor, and are talking of the example of the Carpenter from Nazareth, whom people like me, know as the Son God, you have a character building project before you. You will have to create your own successful person persona, and use it as your intended example.

I don't know where you are going to start. Let me give you one example, and then I will get out of your way. I have hanging on my wall a placard with the heading "The Lombardi Credo." It spells out the thoughts of the former NFL Coach, Vince Lombardi.

He said somewhere or other, "Leaders are made, they are not born; and they are made just like anything else has ever been made in this country - by hard effort. And that's the price that we all have to pay to achieve that goal or any goal."

So you want to be a successful man or woman? Set aside some time: take a pen and a piece of paper and write down what you think a successful person looks like, and then devote your life toward making that kind of person a reality in your life.

Or, as Mr. Groeschel wrote: ". . find what you are looking for."

THIRTY NINE
Significant Act!
Great Results!

We live in a world that is overflowing with Knowledge. If you read a great deal, as I do, you know that much of that wisdom can fall through the cracks and escape our attention.

In his writing "Where Do We Go from Here," Dr. David Jeremiah tells how he and his wife, Donna, confronted the Covid 19 Quarantine in their home. They asked themselves, "When your normal routine is taken away, what do you do? Its easy just to drift along." In a normal situation, it is like asking yourself "When you retire, and no longer have your regular schedule to follow, what do you do? It's easy to just drift along." He went on to say, "We learned the power of doing the next best thing."

Their decision was "We just kept doing the work assigned to us as best we could." In their situation they resolved that though the Pandemic might change the type or intensity of their work, as long as God keeps us on earth, he has jobs for us each day." He then offered these words of J. R. Miller: "We try to settle our duty in large sections. We think of years rather than of moments of life-work rather than of individual acts. It is hard to plan a years duty; it is easy to plan for one short day. No shoulder can bear up the burdens of a years cares - all gathered up, into one load. But the weakest shoulder can carry without weariness - just what reality belongs in just one day."

We will all have to face that time in our lives when we transition from full time work into a new way of living our lives out on a day to day basis. We need to remember, as Dr. Jeremiah noted, that "as long as God keeps us on earth he has jobs for us to do." If you don't believe that God is around, you still have time to fill. The suggestion is that you need to have a plan. It is an important decision. What are you going to do with the rest of your life?

Exercise? It would be easy to just sit around. That would be dangerous to your health. What do you need to do to compensate for your loss of daily activity?

Relationships? Sustaining or making some new relationships? Time with your spouse or children: your new and old friends? Swimming? Golf? Tennis? Cards?

Mental activity? Since I had to read, as part of my professional life, I determined to spend time reading (and writing) each day. Hence these pages! Can you paint?

Why not forget all the results and do the next best thing, - whatever that might be?

I have had friends who, a year into retirement, said: "When did I have time to work?"

As you look forward to the next part of your life, what do you think God has in store for you? What do you have in store for yourself?

FORTY
Do As I Do!

In his writings, Dr. David Jeremiah shares an interesting story about Benjamin Franklin. In his autobiography, he was describing the darkness that filled the streets of Philadelphia in his day. It was pitch black at night and people were stepping into mud puddles and stumbling over rough stones. Even worse, crime was increasing. It wasn't safe to be out after sunset. Franklin waged an intense campaign to persuade everyone to light the area outside their own home, but he got nowhere. Finally he just did it himself - but only in front of his own home. He planted a pole in front of his porch with a kerosene light on top. That night in the city of Philadelphia, there was one house bathed in a warm glow. The lamp cast light on the street, giving passersby a feeling of well-being and safely.

The next night, another house had a lamp, then another. Pretty soon, almost the whole city was lighting the walk ways in front of their houses at night." Jeremiah concluded, "Franklin learned something, that our example is often greater than our admonitions and campaigns."

I think that this is something we all learn very early in our lives. Sadly, it is so simple a truth that we tend to forget it or, at least choose not to remember it, until we grow up; I mean really grow up!.

As Jeremiah noted, it is something that we all must learn: that our example is a very positive thing; a very strong force for good. "Goodness is a quality we can never outlive!"

Enough said? I wonder? Who is looking at you? What did you do yesterday or today that people will remember tomorrow?

FORTY ONE

"The Wiseman Built His House Upon A Rock"

I am having them all of the time: I am now calling them my "Andy Stanley Moments."

I keep asking myself the question he suggested I pose before I make any decision: "Is it the wise thing to do?" The book says it all: "Ask It!" Every day! Any day, I am confronted by it.

I was awakened to the problem many of you will have with it when I came across these words in the Epistle of James: "If any of you lacks wisdom, let him ask of God, who gives to all liberally and without reproach, and it will be given to him." (1:5)

And then these words in Psalm 119: "You, through your commandments, make me wiser than my enemies (for your) words are ever before me." (119:98)

I have no problem with those directives but what about the person who believes that they are alone in this world of ours: who does not have a God they can go too for counsel?? Where do they go for their wisdom? And when they think they get it, how do they know that it is true wisdom?

God is my loadstone. He puts everything in balance for me, - but where do "they" go for guidance? I think it can be very lonely out there. I wonder? Where do you go for that extra amount of wisdom that you need, at those significant moments in your life?

Let me suggest, if you have not yet done this, that you take the necessary time to sit down and determine where YOU go for advice? And maybe more than that: for real honest to goodness wisdom? You might want to try using The Harvard Business School Decision Tree. It seems to work. Maybe it will work for you?

But, how much space do you have on your desk? If you use that mechanism for every decision you have to make, it will take a lot of paper; a whole lot of time. Of course, it will be paper and time well spent.

Achieving your ambitions is no easy task. Don't let the difficulties you face or will face get in your way. Remember the reasons why you started back there in those early years. Keep your ambitions and your life's purpose in mind.

Finding your way in life will require some heavy lifting. I think it was Bob Goff who noted that "the next version of you will pursue the ambitions the previous versions of you were unable to accomplish."

If you are like me, you know it will take a whole lot of praying, - and there will be some mistakes. On the other hand, it will take a whole lot of thinking; of self analysis – and there will be some mistakes. Enjoy the journey!!

FORTY TWO
Where Are You?

In one of his writings ("Dream Big"), Bob Goff suggests that when God asked Adam and Eve, that day in the Garden, following their eating of the apple, "Where are you?", he was referring, not to their geographical location, but to their state of mind. Goff writes, "He wanted to know whether they knew where they were: their state of mind? They were tucked in a bush, yes, but they were really in a place called shame." I am not sure that that was the case but it certainly has some relevance to us living all these years later.

The question Goff believes God was asking our early-on birth parents, as he looked for them in the garden, was "You need to get honest with yourself and determine for yourself just where you are in your life?" As he wrote "Once we figure out where we are, He can lead us from there." "Trust me, heaven will be doing cart wheels if you will finally get real about what you really want."

"It's okay to be somewhere and wish you were in a different spot. ... It's where I am right now," that is important for me to know. It's where I was yesterday. But it is not where I plan to be tomorrow." "Where you are today is simply the harbor from which your ship is about to sail."

I am sure that Mr, Goff was writing to a general audience, so let me narrow it down for an older one. Maybe you can enlist the assistance of someone else. Your age? Your abilities? Your endurance? How about your unfulfilled dreams and aspirations? They all have a place in your decision making process. Where are you?

Goff goes on to say: "When Jesus invited you on this adventure called 'your life', He did it so you could fulfil the ambitions He has for you - to be fully alive and fully His. . . . . He wants you to align your faith with your talents ... He wants you to stare down your fears knowing He has your back and can handle anything that comes your way.

I have a hard time believing that sometimes. Maybe you do to. Well, we are both wrong and short sighted. In Goff's mind, they knew where they were geographicly, but not in their mind's eye. They had some learning to do. And I suspect, so do we.

I like Goff's lay of the land: "Where you are today is simply the harbor from which your ship is about to sale.". Your journey might be just one more day. Or, you might have many days, weeks, or months yet to sail.

To add several of Goff's sentences: "Take the next step.. Don't just look awake: come alive to who God has made you to be. Practice walking around fully awake to yourself." "God never wondered if you had everything you needed to be fully you." He provided you with everything you will need for the journey he has planned for you.

So determine who you are and where you are - and decide where God wants you to go . . . Have a great rest of your journey!

FORTY THREE

The Day I Became A Christian

I was one of the lucky ones! I grew up in a home with Christian parents. I was raised within the framework of the Christian faith. In the words of one revolutionary era pastor, whose name has passed me by, "I never knew when I was not a Christian."

The situation has posed a number of problems for me. In a way, I have always envied those individuals who moved from "the dark side" of life to the "sonny side." And when people would ask me about my Christian experience, I had nothing but a very bland explanation. Certainly nothing to write home about.

I had just finished reading Lee Strobels book, "The Case For Grace;" the stories of a variety of individuals who had made the transition from a "none" Christian life to a grace filled, faith experience when I came across a story, in a book of daily readings, that satisfied my need and provided me with an answer to that cumbersome question, "When were you saved?"

The writer wrote, "When a questioner tried to pin down (the famed) theologian Karl Barth on when he had been saved," Barth replied, "It happened one afternoon in A.D. 34 when Jesus died on the cross." That was the day I, too, had been saved, and I will remember it always. Go ahead ask me. "When were you saved?" "It happened one afternoon in A.D. 34 when Jesus died on the cross."

And I have lived a grace filled life ever since!

It was that same Karl Barth who, when asked to share the essence of the Christian faith, replied:

> "Jesus loves me, this I know; cause the Bible tells me so,
> I am weak, but he is strong, ...
> Yes, Jesus loves me, Yes, Jesus loves me,
> Cause the Bible tells me so."

FORTY FOUR

The Importance Of Looking Forward

I remember reading the story of Franklin Jacobs, a short guy with a powerful set of legs. A high jumper, a number of years ago, he jumped seven feet, seven and a half inches; that is twenty three and a fourth inches over his head. He had an unusual style, the kind a coach would normally seek to change. When someone said something to his coach about it, he quipped; "When you jump that high, you don't have to worry about style."

Dr. Phillip Hench discovered cortisone. He was an obstetrician. In the course of time he discovered that pregnant women naturally produced a lot of cortisone through their adrenal system and that it reduced the problems of arthritis. It took him twelve years to synthesize his discovery. On top of that, it took him seven more years to prove his point in the large regimen of modern science. That is a long time in anyone's life. No one was shouting, "Long live, Dr. Hench!" There were no cheerleaders or encouragers; just the expenditure of time, energy and anticipation. But he was true to his course, When he was tempted to quit; when he was tired; when he was disappointed, when he was castigated - all those things that happen to great men and women who keep surviving, even when things don't go right, he kept moving in a forward direction.

How important it is to believe in the possibilities that are within us and about us. Think of all the forlorn people around us in our world. How tempted they are to quit.

Remember the story of the prophet, Elisha, in the book of Second Kings? (Chapter 6) He and his sidekick found themselves in the village of Dothan. The servant awoke one morning to find he and his Master surrounded by the army of the King of Syria. When he finally awakened the prophet and apprised him of their situation, the Prophet said to him, "Don't be afraid! We have more on our side than they have on their's." Then he said to God: "Open his eyes and let him see what I mean." And immediately the eyes of the servant revealed that the Syrian army was surrounded by an angelic host, swords unsheathed, and the power of the Almighty around them.

(The Hymn "Open Our Eyes," comes to mind.)

And so, with each one of us, - because our God stands in the wings waiting for us to open our eyes to catch a glimpse of his presence. Yes, we can face our future, no matter how bleak it may seem to be. There are so many around us, ready and willing to help us in our times of need.

Someone says: "Let's look up! Not down. Let's look forward and not backward!" "Let's look out and around, and not within. Let's realize that we are a part of the "Army of the Almighty," and nothing, nothing can keep us from going and doing what God intends for us to go and do! Let us center the remaining days, weeks, months and years of our lives, knowing beyond the shadow of any doubt, that God is here, right here - with us.

So, as you continue your journey, no matter what your situation, your status, your physical or financial situation, remember the words of the prophet: "You got a lot more going for you, than you ever dreamed of."

Remember! Never forget. God has your back!

FORTY FIVE

Life's Most Important Question/Answer

It was a question I never had to answer. My parents did it for me. As I mentioned in an earlier writing, they provided me with an answer before I was ever asked the question. They raised me in a Christian home, so I never knew what it was like to not live in a Christian environment. But there are a good many people out there who have to answer the question for themselves, without parental help or involvement. Maybe you are one of them. I don't care who you are; no matter what your religious beliefs; if anything, you can't just ignore this question and move on.

I was prompted to bring the question up as I read the first several chapters of Charles Stanley's writing, which he entitled "The Will of God." He writes. ". . if no one has ever had the joyful privilege of helping you to receive Christ's gift of salvation . . All it takes is being willing to admit that you cannot overcome your sin on your own, but that you trust that the sacrifice Jesus made on the Cross was sufficient to forgive everything you have ever done wrong. If so, you can tell him in your own words, using this simple prayer:

> **Lord Jesus, I come to you asking you to forgive my sins and save me from eternal separation from God. In faith, I accept your work and death on the cross as sufficient payment for my transgressions. I also confess that you are Lord. Help me to turn from my sins and live in a manner that is pleasing to you.**

I praise you for providing me the way for me to know You and to have a relationship with my heavenly Father. Through faith in You, I have eternal life and I trust You have prepared a home for me. I acknowledge trusting You as my Savior is my first step into understanding and living out God's will.

Thank You for hearing my prayers, loving me unconditionally, and leading me to God's plan. Please give me the strength, wisdom and determination to walk in the center of Your will. In Jesus' name. Amen.

I hope that you can pray this simple prayer. If not, please keeping about it and move on into the rest of your life. Eternity is not very far away from us. We are almost there. I want you to be ready for it, having considered ALL the other options.

FORTY SIX

What Do You Want Out Of Life?

I n the introduction to his book "Counterfeit Gods," Tim Keller shares this thought from the Frenchman Alexis De Tocqueville, in the 1830's. He wrote that Americans believed, in those days, that prosperity could quench their yearning for happiness, but such a hope was illusory because the "incomplete joys of this world will never satisfy (the human) heart." This strange melancholy manifests itself in many way but always leads to the same despair; of not finding what is sought.

And what is this "strange melancholy" that permeates our society even during the boom times of frenetic activity, and which turns to outright despair when prosperity diminishes? De Tocqueville surmises that it comes from taking "some incomplete joy of this world" and building your entire life on it." Sound familiar?

We are living in a time when money and power are on the minds of almost every one of our leaders. They are afraid of each other and they are afraid of going in any other direction, for fear of being left out or left behind. Go ahead. Tell me I am wrong?

And what about you? How many of us don't want more? And our kids even want more! Who will you vote for at the next election, if you even have a choice?

I think it was Madonna who remarked: ". . even though I have become somebody, I still have to prove that I'm Somebody. My struggle never ends and it probably never will." Does that maybe remind you of yourself? And in the movie "Chariots Of Fire," the main character sighs: "Contentment! I'm twenty four and I've never known it. I'm forever in pursuit and I don't even know what it is I'm chasing." A counselor by the name of Mary Bell sizes up the situation in these words: "Achievement is the alcohol of our time." How long does it take for us to realize this fallacy in our makeup, and when the truth suddenly dawns upon us, how long will it take for us to do anything about it, - even if we really try?

If we want to get a real grip on our lives we have got to find some bedrock to build on. As far as I am personally concerned, that bed rock is God and what he has to say about life: about my life. Frankly, I have no other ideas. If you have some, try them out, and if those ideas fail, you will have to go back to the beginning and start out all over again.

Keller reflects: "Mature Christians are not people who completely hit the bedrock. I don't believe that is possible in this life. Rather, they are people who know how to keep drilling and are getting closer and closer."

Any day, every day, we need to take stock of our lives. Are we satisfied with who we are and what we are doing. Do we have objectives; goals that we can possibly achieve or are whatever dreams we have out of the reach of our abilities and opportunities? At some point in our lives we need to become realistic. What can we do today or tomorrow that will touch our lives or the lives of another in a very positive way?

Is that, maybe, what we ought to be looking for; striving to do.

FORTY SEVEN
The Power Of One

Kyle Idelman reminds us in his recent book "One At Time," that Jesus conducted a "one person at a time" ministry. He preached to hundreds and thousands, but, on the whole, he dealt with one person at a time. You know some of the individuals on his list of accomplishments: the woman at the well, the rich young ruler, Lazarus, Peter, the woman accused of adultery. He makes this assumption: ". . wherever God has placed you is a space in which He wants to use you." Then this challenge: "Maybe we need to stop leaning into the usual ways this world tells us to measure difference-making and start leaning into the unexpected ways God wants to use us."

Mother Teresa, the famed Nun from Calcutta, was asked one day, what special qualities allowed her to make such a massive impact on society. Her response: "I don't claim anything of the work. I am like a little pencil in his hand, that is all. He does the thinking. He does the writing. The pencil has nothing to do with it. The pencil has only to be used."

She told of a man who was living in absolute squalor. She told him that she was going to clean his house, wash his windows, and make his bed. While cleaning the house she discovered a lamp that was covered with dust. She asked the man: "Don't you light your lamp? Don't you ever use it? He answered, "No! No one comes to see me. I have no need to light it."

She asked him if he would light it if the local nuns came to visit. He replied, "Of course." That day the nuns committed to visiting him every evening. Two years later,

Mother Teresa said she had completely forgotten that man, until she received a message from him. It said: "Tell my friend that the light she lit in my life continues to shine still!"

That's the power of one!

I wonder who, in your life's landscape, God is waiting for you to touch! Whose light can you turn on: whose life could you change with just one act or word? Look around! Someone is out there "waiting."

Look in one of your mirror's. Think of the positive power you have to turn someone's world around? Whose lamp can you light?

You have power. One person power. Use it!

FORTY EIGHT

The Importance Of Your Light In The World

While doing some mining work in Max Lucado's book on The Holy Spirit "Help Is Here," I came across this wonderful story that speaks to everyone of us, no matter what our age, color or faith: It is a fable "about a dying father and his three sons. Having given his life to building a company, it was time turn it over to one of them.. But which one? The father had a plan. He called them to his bedside and handed a dollar bill to each young man and gave them this assignment: 'Buy something that fills the room. The one who takes up the most space will be entrusted with the company.'

Each of the boys obeyed the instruction. The first returned with two bales of hay that he purchased for fifty cents a piece. They covered the floor of the room. The second purchased two feather pillows, cut them open, and let the feathers fill the air. The father was pleased but not satisfied. He turned to the third son and asked, 'What did you do with your dollar?'

The boy had nothing in his hands, so he explained I gave fifty cents to an orphanage, twenty cents to a church and twenty cents to a soup kitchen.'

One of his siblings objected, 'But he did nothing to fill up the room.'

'Yes, I did' the boy exclaimed. I spent the last dime on two items.' He reached into his pocket and took out a little matchbook and candle. He lit the candle and turned off the light switch. From corner to corner the candle filled the room, not with hay or feathers, but with light."

Lucado then finished the chapter with this question: "With what are you filling your world?"

I was almost immediately reminded of the song that George Beverly Shea used to sing at the Billy Graham Evangelistic Crusades. "This Little Light Of Mine, I'm Going To Let It Shine." And that act is so important in our world today. How many places, circumstances and conversations would be changed and blessed by a little bit of "positive light?"

The Roman Catholic priest, Richard Rohr tells of a conversation he had with the South African clergyman Desmond Tutu. The Bishop had this to say: "We are only the light bulbs. Our job is to remain screwed in." Rohr went on to say: "The light comes from elsewhere yet it is necessarily reflected (through those still walking on the journey.)"

The Carpenter from Nazareth said, in his famed "Sermon on the Mount:" "You are like light for the whole world. A city built on a hill cannot be hid. No one lights a lamp and puts it under a bowl; instead he puts it on a lampstand, where it gives light for everyone in the house. In the same way your light must shine before people . ." (Matthew 5:14-16)

That's an important assignment to each one of us: "to shine!" What were the opening words to that old Gospel song: "Brighten The Corner Where You Are!" Are you shining where you are? If not, you have got some work to do.....

FORTY NINE

Never Forget: Never Give Up!

It was a short little paragraph. It contained only two sentences. One was a question? The other was an answer to that question and a lesson we all must learn. The question: "Do you realize that one of the largest veins of gold ever discovered in America was found only three feet from where previous miners had stopped digging?" And the answer was and is: ". . (We all) "experience the same problem, as to just where we quit. Possibly just out of reach from where we ought to be willing to go," we will find the answer to a situation before us.. Let me be honest with you. The author of the question was writing to what he supposed was a Christian audience: his answer was: **"Christians often experience the same problems: just beyond where we quit, just out of reach from where we are willing to Go, is Gods greatest blessing."** What I am attempting to say is that this is a situation we all will encounter.

You will, perhaps remember, that Winston Churchill was asked to speak to the Commencement class of a boy's school in Great Britain. When he was called to the lectern, he spoke these words to the graduates, "Newer Give Up! Newer Give Up! Never Give Up! And he sat down.

Wow!

Let's face it. As with so many other situations in life, - this is an attitude problem. YOU are the primary person in these situations. It all has to do with whom YOU bring to the table. Who are you? How strong are you, emotionally speaking. How long are you willing to stand the line? Can you stand up for yourself? Is what YOU believe, what you really believe?

I think it all begins with how you get up in the morning. With what convictions do you begin your day? Are you as strong today as you were yesterday; last night, before you closed your eyes in sleep? Do you set your eyes toward the horizon and your feet fully planted in what you think and say YOU believe, before you have your final cup of coffee and run out the door?

How positive is your attitude? How strong are your convictions? How patient can you be? Are you? The world is waiting for more convicted, strong will people to live and act in it.

Today! Out there in your world! Stand tall! Never give up on your intended goals or aspirations! Never!

FIFTY

Always Keep The End In Sight

D r. David Jeremiah has a unique but challenging ending to his book, "Where Do We Go From Here." It is to be found in the New Testament book of Colossians; in chapter four, at verse seventeen. He writes, "It's a personal message addressed to one individual; To you. . . . Actually, it's to a man named Archippas, but you can put your name in that spot. It says, 'Take heed to the ministry which you have received in the Lord, that you may fulfill it.' In other words, finish the work. Complete the task. Make sure by the end of your life, you also come to the end of your (self)-assigned earthly work."

Jeremiah goes on to say, ". . . God (Life) has given you certain gifts . . certain tasks. Make sure you complete them. We don't have to get out of this world alive," but we should expect to complete the work we started out to do.

So, think back to the early years; what were your dreams; your aspirations? What did you want to do with your life? Now, as it is drawing to a close, think about it: did you satisfy those goals: did you change them or alter them? Did you satisfy those adjusted dreams and aspirations? Where are you now? Where do you want to be? What do you still have to do to get your planned life's goals accomplished? Are you going to be satisfied, on your death bed, that you achieved all you set out to do? Wow! That is a heavy assignment, but did you get your job or jobs done? And if you didn't, what can you do to finish them off? Or, can you pass on your goal to someone else, and know they will finish what you started?

Maybe you could put your assessment in your last will and testament. Maybe, like the letters that Ex-Presidents leave in their desk, in the oval office, you can leave a message in your desk drawer in your place of employment, at home in your office; anywhere the person you have in mind might get it.

Where do your ideas or goals go from here?

FIFTY ONE
The Ultimate Importance Of Belief

It has been said that "**Belief** is the single most important thing about us: that our beliefs are far more important than our bank accounts, our reputation, or our schooling. Successful crooks have large bank accounts, undetected hypocrites have glowing reputations, and highly educated people pursue evil ends." "Belief should be the all involving act of our lives."

Now the author of those words was a Protestant minister. He had a particular point of view in mind: God should be the center of our attention.

But what about those who find themselves standing outside the realm of religious thinking? The world, today is full of people who, if they don't deny the existence of God, certainly don't allow the thought of him to prey on their thinking. Maybe you are one of them.

Well, I guess we need to start here. What do you believe in? What might be your answer?

I believe in God!

I believe in. . . . .

I believe in . . . .

I believe in myself!

Now you have the opportunity to fill in the blank space.

Did you write down who you believe in? What you believe in! There is a significant distance between "believing in God" and "believing in your self." But you have got to believe in someone or something. So what's your answer?

It's a question that is to be found on many pages of this writing and its predecessor. Sorry! But it is the prime question on which to base your life. There is not much you really can do, that will not bother you, until you have a firm hold on your answer. If you can believe and declare "I believe in God!" you can begin to consider where you are along life's way. If you come up with any other answer, stop where you are; answer the question for yourself and then hop back on your life's road.

Until you have the answer to the question, you will always wonder about what you said and did I do the right thing? Did I say the right thing? Am I going in the right direction?

Well? Have you got your thoughts firmly under control? Here's that Andy Stanley question again. "Is what I am doing? Is what I am saying, the wise thing to do or say?

What do you believe? Who do you believe in?

FIFTY TWO

The Importance of those "Stop For A Minute" Moments

In his book "Can You Still Trust God," Charles Stanley reminds us of these important words of Dr. James Packer on the subject of "Meditation:" "Meditation is the activity of calling to mind, and thinking over, and dwelling on, and applying to oneself, the various things that one knows about the works, and purposes and promises of God. It is an activity of holy thought, consciously performed in the presence of God, under the eye of God, by the help of God, as a means of communion of God. Its purpose is to clear one's mental and spiritual vision of God, and to let his truth make its full and proper impact on ones mind and heart. It is a matter of talking to oneself about God and oneself; it is, indeed, often a matter of arguing with oneself out of moods of doubt and unbelief into a clear apprehension of God's power and grace."

It is a matter of standing before oneself and considering the state of one's mind and beliefs in the light of what we know to be God's truth. I need to apprehend where I am in the light of where I have been, before I seek to go ahead with all of my planned activities..

Often in my writings I suggest that one stop and reflect on where we are before we move on to the next minutes in our life. This could happen every day, every week; anytime we feel uncertain about our future; maybe every hour. It means to live a cautious life. The older we get the more often we need to sit down and consider our situation. "The important thing is that we get alone with the Lord to find his direction and purpose for our lives."

As Stanley notes: "The essence of meditation is a period of time set aside to contemplate the Lord, listen to him, allow him to permeate our spirits. When we do something happens within us that equips us to carry out our duties . . . Whatever we do, the time of meditation is God's time of equipping us in preparation for life.:" "Private meditation allows the Lord Jesus Christ to have each of us all to himself. His private workings are often His most precious."

Proverbs 8:34 exclaims, "Blessed is the (man) who listens to me . ." "Meditation brings us to a position in which we can see ourselves in the light of God's truth."

So maybe its time for you to slow down and take a few minutes to catch up with yourself before you move on to the next phase in your life?

So Stop! Wherever you are. Whatever you are doing. Stop right now!

FIFTY THREE

We Don't Need To Be Perfect: Just Keep Trying!

I have been following the daily reading schedule shared by Philip Yancey in his book "Grace Notes." One of his selections was entitled "World Without God." He begins by quoting Vaclay Havel, the former president of the Czech Republic, who offered up this thought: "I believe that with the loss of God, man has lost a kind of absolute and universal system of coordinates to which he could always relate everything, chiefly himself. His world and his personality gradually began to break up into separate incoherent fragments corresponding to different, relative coordinates."

Yancey makes this observation: "We live in dangerous times and face urgent questions not only about the environment, but also about terrorism, war, sexuality world poverty and definitions of life and death." Society badly needs a moral tether, or 'system of coordinates.' in Havel's phrase. We need to know our place in the universe and our obligation to each other and to the earth. Can we answer those questions without God?" As far as Yancey is concerned, the answer was "No!"

The question then becomes, "What do we do about it?" The answer is, we need to get God back into the system and we do that by engaging ourselves, personally, in acts of evangelism." We begin to talk about God: about who God is; about how he acts! Eugene Peterson suggests that most people have too little knowledge about God. They don't know that God is for them: that he is right beside them. "And they don't know the way and are wasting their lives hunting and pecking, guessing and groping, hoping that they will get lucky some day with a lottery ticket to heaven."

As Peterson says: ". as Christians we know that God is for us and know the way to receive him in Jesus Christ. We don't know' everything about (the) great issues, but we know at least that much. And we know that it is both our obligation and our joy to tell others." Who have you told about God recently: about Jesus Christ: about his love and grace?

I must admit that I am too often mum on the subject. I live in a retirement community and have been afraid to offend somebody about something or anything. I have got to grow up and get involved in speaking out about the presense of God. How?

I believe it was the famed English author, G. K. Chesterton, whom I know through reading his mysteries involving Father Brown, in a book, now lost to me, who wrote: "If anything is worth doing, it is worth doing badly." Applying it to the act of evangelism, it means that I must try to be an evangelist. How?

Well, my first attempt is to begin to witness for my God and his Christ at the food table, I have always prayed before our meals at home but have always shied away from doing it in restaurants and in the company of other people. Beginning to day that will change.

God is alive and well and he will publicly be thanked for my meal tonight and at every meal that comes my way. What about your "Coming Out Party?" How are you going to get God back into the system?

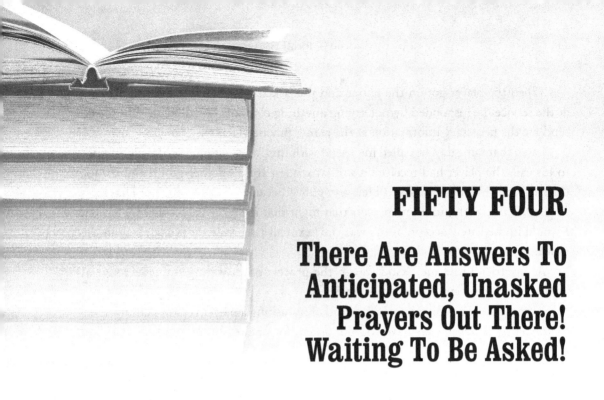

FIFTY FOUR

There Are Answers To Anticipated, Unasked Prayers Out There! Waiting To Be Asked!

I remembered, the other night, the experience of a friend that I had almost forgotten. He was the member of a community ministerial group that was planning a Baccalaureate Service. In their discussion, it was pointed out that they were having a hard time getting boys involved in that "volunteer service." How would they get the boys to attend. They decided that they would need an athlete of some importance, to get the boy's attention. My friend was asked to give an invitation to a member of an NFL team..

They chose a player, and he called the Team Headquarters for his phone number. The Team said that they could not give out the number, without the player's approval. So he wrote the Team and explained the reason for the request. Several weeks later he received their written reply, and was asked to once again call the team office.

He called and they gave him the player's Home phone (This was before the creation of the cell phone.) They also told him that the player had left his home, in the west, and was driving to the East Coast for a required practice. They noted a place he would be that night.

The next morning, at seven a.m., he called the number before he realized that the time zone into which he was calling was three hours behind his time. He couldn't hang up once the motel had answered his call so he waited to speak his apology.

When the player got on the phone and was asked if he would consider speaking at the service, he responded by not saying anything else but, "I will be glad to speak; send me the necessary information at the team's practice facility.

Later, that same day, he called my friend with this information. On the night, prior to his call, the player had received a similar request from another group and turned them down. That night, he said, "I felt very guilty, because" he said, "the Lord has been so good to me. So I said in my prayers that night that if I received another invitation, I would immediately accept. Yours was the next call I received (at four o'clock in the morning.).

As my friend told me, "God was in the process of answering my prayer several weeks before the event happened." Wow!!

It set me to wondering, how long ahead of my asking a prayer is God making plans to answer it? What prayers have you not asked, for one reason or another, that God was (is) ready to answer?

FIFTY FIVE
Things I Didn't Know I Knew

In recent days I have learned that there are many things in life that I knew about that I didn't know I knew. I don't wish to sound arrogant; I just want to be truthful. What I mean is that as I reflect on the writings of other people, and write down what I think they mean, in the things they wrote, I find myself giving expression to things that I know and believe.

This thought dawned upon me as I read some words in Eugene H. Peterson's writings in "On Living Well," put together by another writer. Peterson wrote: "Language is the means by which what is unknown and what is hidden becomes accessible." He then goes on to say: "Language - this wonderful gift, this mysterious capacity that we have to say who we are, to bring out into the open the secrets of our hearts, the nuances of our emotions, and the thoughts whether confused or clear in our minds - is our basic means for working out who we are by answering God, responding to his invitations and commands."

This thought would suggest that our minds are a treasure trove of wisdom waiting to be tapped, at any time, for the encouragement and benefit of other people. What treasures are stored up in your mind that could be brought to light by your reflecting on what you read and running it through the thought processes of your mind? What benefits could you glean from the thoughts of others, as you run them through your mind and imprint your personality on them?

May be we don't take what we read seriously enough or read it through to its desired end. I wonder, is it just stored up somewhere in there, waiting to be exposed and given a new life?

In those same paragraphs Peterson adds: "God uses language to bring into being his will. His will is now evident to us . . . "We see and hear it all around us, (these) consequences of God's speaking:", in nature, in our acts of faith, in love and mercy. "And in return we speak to God," and to each other. What are we holding back by not thinking through the thoughts that come to us through others?

We need to remember that we are not "the end" that God has in mind; but a means toward that end!

Use all of your mind! Use it all of the time! Who knows what God can do with what he has allowed you to store up in it?. Think about it now. What truths are inside of you, waiting to get out?

FIFTY SIX

Do We Always Have To Change?

Do we always have to change our way of thinking or our attitude? I hope not. Sometimes I don't want to change.

During my adult growing up years, right up until now, at age eighty eight, in the east and midwest, prior to the beginning of the formal worship service, on Sunday mornings, the organist played the prelude, and people took their seats and sat in silence, in preparation for worship. Today, in the west, on Sunday mornings, the time before the formal service begins is noisy, like before a sporting event. You can hardly think straight. It seems to bother nobody but me. I don't know what God makes of it. It probably doesn't bother Him. However, I yearn for some quiet. Help!

In his book "One At A Time," Kyle Idelman takes issue with me. He writes: "Christianity is the haunting fear that someone, somewhere, is having a good time." Then he adds: "We need to give people a different view of who Jesus is, by giving them a different view of who we are as his followers. Not because a joyless Christianity misrepresents Jesus and the will of God but because a joyless Christianity is unattractive." (So we should be noisy before worship, like at a basketball game?)

I don't believe that to be true at all. Quietness produces reverence. People don't know what it means to be reverent before worship. The "noise" turns me off, even if God welcomes it. So, I sit there, somewhat disgusted and put off, and try to listen to the prelude; whether it is being played on the organ, or plumbed on a guitar. (I liked to hear the organ.)

I long for a bit of quietness, so I can think about my relationship with God and my neighbor. The music is a blessing, not an interruption. And I know that I will probably not get that quiet time again, in my lifetime. It is lost to a noisy age. But I think that God is there, waiting in the noise, to hear from me. So I will keep trying to talk with him.

I will not change. There is more to my faith than just coming to a Sunday morning party. The changing of the water to wine, at the wedding at Cana in Galilee happened quietly. Only the servants really knew what happened. Only I know what happens when I worship. - And God!

FIFTY SEVEN
Determining What's Important

I n one of his writings, Eugene H. Peterson, the man responsible for "The Message" (translation of the Bible) wrote: Our opinions and arguments on world affairs make nothing happen, but several times a day, we have chances at peacemaking, praying, and loving that implement the kingdom of God." Our routines accumulate debris - things we once needed and don't anymore, activities that began as essentials and now produce needless fatigue. We need seasonal house cleanings, otherwise we buy too much and run around too much. Wise Christians get rid of whatever is interfering with who we want to be before God and with each other. Wise Christians go back to the basics."

Frankly, I don't know what wise Christians do, but I know, for sure, that those words speak words that I need to hear and act on. The older we get, the more baggage we accumulate and as the years mount up, the more cumbersome of those things, we think about and do, burden us.

There has to be a time: there have to be many times, as our years mount up, that we have to rethink what is going on in our lives, and the reasons behind those actions. And that is no easy task because the valid reasons behind those thoughts and actions are ingrained into the very fabric of our lives. They are reasoned and right. Their only problem is that our life has changed and so we have to see how yesterdays rules and regulations need to be rethought and refigured into today's worlds.

Now I do not know what of "yesterdays rules and regulations" need to be rethought and refigured. As I suggested in "Reflection #1" I do not feel that life's basic rules never change. They always stand firm and tall. It is my own personal thoughts and feelings that need to be reassessed. I can buy into that, wholeheartedly. That is, we need to take some time aside, and look at how we are living the way we are, and why we have been living that way. Professionally and privately we need to look at our attitudes and actions and determine what is keeping us there.

The rules that guide my life: my theological convictions; my staff philosophy, how I deal with family and friends; my negative attitudes toward certain people: they all need to be revisited and adjusted where necessary. Like cleaning out the drawers in your kitchen, your desk and your car. (My Dad used to say that you can judge a person by the state of their car trunk. I never forgot that bit of wisdom.)

Now this probably ought to be a weekly or monthly routine because things can quickly get out of hand. So, you figure out where you are and where you ought to be. Nobody can do it for you.

So, Get ready; Get set! GO!

Now, what will the new YOU look like? Act?

FIFTY EIGHT
Out Of The Many: Be Careful!

Somebody says they figured it out; that we speak about sixteen thousand words per day. They write: "Sixteen thousand words a day is like writing a sixty page book every day with the words you speak. And each of those words matters." They add: "Our worlds are created by the words spoken to us, and with our words we create the world around us." And the conclusion he reached; and I am talking about the man who wrote those words, was Kyle Idelman. He wrote: "We need to understand that words have the power of life and death and start choosing them carefully." And that is a mouthful of words, to say the least. What kind of history did you make with the words that you spoke today?

Yes, the words that we speak have a great deal of power in them. We can use them to build people up or destroy them. His awareness of the importance of the words we speak led Paul to write to his friends in Ephesus: "Let no unwholesome word proceed from your mouth, but only such a word as is good for edification according to the need of the moment, so that it will give grace to those who hear." (Eph 4:29)

Thinking about the words that we speak, and how we utter them so uselessly, Idelman remarked: "If we want to live and love like Jesus (and no human being, no matter what their faith may be, could not want less than that), we need to understand that words have the power of life and death, and start choosing them carefully."

I am reminded of a Children's Junior Sermon that I heard, and then told myself a number of times. The object was a tube of toothpaste. If you squeezed it, the contents came out; however, if you got too much on your brush, you could not get it back in the tube. It was out to stay; you could not put it back. And the point: once you speak, you cannot take your words back: they are out in the world to stay - to do harm or good.

We need to be careful in our choice of words; really careful. And in this world today, where people talk too much, and lie too often, that is especially true.

Somewhere I read of someone who, every evening before they went to sleep, looked back on their conversations during the day, noting what they had said to anyone and everyone, and determined who they should contact the next day, to apologize for some loose word they had spoken to them.

Today! Tonight! Tomorrow morning! Reflect on the words you spoke today. What shouldn't you have said? Did you say too much? Get right with the people you know and love before you move on!

It's never too late to start! So start right now!

FIFTY NINE
The Value Of The Rear View Mirror

I have often read of the Chinese philosopher who road backwards on a donkey because he believed that we can only understand life by looking backward..

There is something to be said for that, because it is one way to see how God has been active in your life. As I look back on my life, as I have experienced it, and plot out how I arrived at where I am, in the light of how I got there, I can see, graphically, how God has guided and directed me to where I now am. Yes, God has been "active" in my life.

I cannot comprehend what has happened to me, or why, until I am ready to acknowledge that God is a moving force in my life. I do not know what he will do tomorrow, but I can see what he did yesterday. Only then can I anticipate his presence in my tomorrow.

With that awareness in mind, I can turn my head around and face tomorrow and look for the opportunities that are right in front of me. Confident that he has been active in my past, now I know that he will be active in my todays and tomorrows. Bob Goff says of this experience: "It's about developing a greater awareness of what is already happening around us and showing up for it with a boatload of joy and anticipation." God is alive and well, ready to do new things for us and because of us."

Looking through the rear view mirror is a faith builder. It tells us what God can do and what he is capable of doing, if we are willing to be led by him. Philip Yancey sums it up with these words "What is faith, after all, but believing in advance what will only make sense in reverse."

Again, in the words of Mr. Goff: "How many days remain for you? . . . Who will you decide to be, and what will you decide to do with the time you have left?" Friend, that is your decision; you have to make it. So, get with it!

Once you have become aware of what God has already done in your life; now it is time to reach out and determine what else he can do. Was it not the late evangelist D. L. Moody who said, "The world is yet to see what God can do with a soul completely dedicated to him?" Moody thought he was a man like that. Are you ready to be another?

SIXTY

One Good Act At A Time

As the extended Bibliography in this book might suggest, I read a great deal.. As I troll through a good many books, looking for exciting thoughts that might escape the thoughts of many others; I feel compelled to pause and re-examine them. Sentences, paragraphs and other extended thoughts that, if examined, possess ideas that will provide us insights into how to live out our lives, particularly in our later years.. They just seem to pass people by; I find them, - and seek to pass them on.

One of those thoughts is found in a book by Pastor, TV Preacher and author Dr. David Jeremiah. In a book published several years ago Dr. Jeremiah provides us with a thoughtful paragraph from a writing of Craig Brian Larson.

Dr. Jeremiah was reminding us of the importance that Jesus attached to the act of sharing our love with those who come into our lives.

Larson wrote: "We think giving our all to the Lord is like taking a 1000 dollar bill and laying it on the table (saying) - "Here's my life, Lord. I'm giving it all!" We read of individuals who leave a waitress or waiter a large tip, before departing the restaurant, or someone contributing a significant amount of money to one charity or another.

However Larson continues: "But the reality for most of us is that he sends us to the bank and has us cash in the $1000. for quarters. We go through life putting our 25 cents here, 50 cents there. Listening to the neighbor kids troubles instead of saying, "Get lost!" Going to a Committee meeting. Giving a cup of water to a shaky old man in a nursing home.

Then he adds: "Usually giving our life to Christ isn't glorious. It's done in all those little acts of love, 25 cents at a time." And Jeremiah concludes: "It's lived out in small, everyday ways over the course of a lifetime." Or, in the words of the disciple John, "Beloved, let us love one another, for love is of God; and everyone who loves is born of God and knows God." (I John 4r:7)

There are very few of us who have a thousand dollars to give away, but how about 25 cents or a dollar?

Twenty Five Cents! Fifty Cents! One Dollar! Five Dollars!

A simple "Thank You!" A "Get Well" Card! Just a computer sent "Greeting Card!" A "Tip" for a Waitress or Waiter! A "Bereavement" Card! A "Wave Of The Hand!" A "Toot" of the Car Horn!" Oh, so many ways - all to say you care!

Today has so many opportunities! Tomorrow has so many possibilities. For YOU!

SIXTY ONE
A Pattern For Coping

There is an old legend of how birds got their wings. According to that legend, the little birds didn't have wings, at first, so they would just scamper about on the ground. But one day God got worried about them. So, that night, while the birds were asleep, God attached wings to their sides.

The next morning, when the little birds woke up they felt burdened and bothered by those heavy, cumbersome things attached to their sides: they felt awkward and weighted down. It was very difficult for them to move about. Those wings were a nuisance. They complained and fussed and felt sorry for themselves. But then some of the little birds began to move their wings, and they were surprised at how graceful it felt. They exercised their wings and then suddenly some of them began to fly. Soon others also began to try it and they also found themselves flying.

Now the point of the legend is obvious, I think. It contains a beautiful lesson for life, namely this; what seemed at first to be a heavy, great burden to the little birds became their means of flight, the means by which they could soar into the skies above them.

Friends - our problems can become opportunities. Our problems can become the means by which we can soar into a higher level, a higher level of maturity and a higher level of faith. With the help of God; with God on our side, we can cope, and so we can know that we can live a triumphant life, today!

We are called to move through our problems, not around them - not away from them but through them. So it is important that we learn and know that we are not walking alone; that God is walking with us; that we come to know what he is like and what he wishes for us. Friends: that knowledge will change your life! You can count on it!

SIXTY TWO

Keeping The Act Of Forgiveness Under Control

I was reading a book by James Bryan Smith entitled "The Good And Beautiful You." In it, he speaks of a college mentor who offered this word of advice to him: "'Keep short accounts with God,' which meant everytime I sinned I needed to confess right away, so as to 'clear the account..' He said the secret to Christian living was what he called 'spiritual breathing.' When he sinned he breathed out his confession. "Forgive me, God for that thought," and then he breathed in God's forgiveness. 'Thank you Lord, for hearing my confession and forgiving my sin.'"

As I have confessed innumerable times, years ago, about forty live years ago. I spoke some uncalled-for words to a friend, who then became less than a friend. Instead of putting things right with him, I let the situation pass. Now, I am still paying the price for those unnecessary words.

I am sure God forgave me. My old friend couldn't because I never told him, "I was sorry" for speaking them. And I have never ever forgiven myself! And I hurt because of it.

If I had known of Dr. Smith's Mentors advice, and acted on it, I could think of my former friend, positively, and not with regret.

I never understood much of what Dr. Paul Tillich said or wrote, but I do remember these words: "Forgiveness is remembering the past in order that it might be forgotten."

I share Dr. Smith's advice and the words of Dr. Tillich with you, in hopes that you might not make the same mistake I did. Frankly, it is great advice. I pray that you will heed these words, starting now!

Who is waiting to hear from you? What relationships can you mend today?

SIXTY THREE
Wake Up Your Dreams

I t was one of those human interest stories, about a forty seven year old man. It was titled, "One Man's Life Of No Regrets!" It told its readers that at the age of 15, the man had set out 127 things that he wanted to accomplish during his lifetime. He had accomplished 105 of them. It reported him as saying that he now had the rest of his life to reach out and grab the remaining 22.

Helen Keller was once asked, "What would be worse than being born blind?" Her reply was: "To have sight and have no vision.

The problem with too many people is that when they realize what it would cost to dream a dream and carry out a vision, they determine that it would be much easier to go with the flow, and do what's expected of them, and no more. It's a state of mind that can creep up on us without our ever knowing it.

Somewhere I was made aware of the fact that one of the mountains in the Alps that is particularly popular with climbers has a "Rest House" about halfway up its summit. The owner of the house once remarked that a rather interesting phenomenon happens, on a regular basis. That is, when some climbers get into the house and begin to warm up, they give in to the temptation to stop climbing. They say to their companions, "You know, I think I will just wait here while you finish your climb. When you get back here, we can just head down together."

As they wait, a sense of satisfaction comes over them, as they sit by the fire, staying warm, listening to the piano, and singing mountain climbing songs. After their companions leave, and continue their climb, a calm quiet seems to dominate the room, even as some of them go to a window to see if they can see their friends continuing their climb. The owner's comment was, "You see, suddenly they begin to realize that they have settled for that which is second best and that only those who were willing to pay the price will reach their original, intended goal."

Someone has suggested that they believe God is waiting and willing to reveal to each and every one of them, things that could radically change their lives and, perhaps, change the world around them. They said they believed that God is eternally waiting to call out of us something that has never been said or thought of, since the beginning of time. It was the columnist David Brooks who reflected that he writes, in part "to remind myself of the kind of life I want to live," - and I, personally, agree whole heartedly with that.

Most of us, at some point in our lives, have sensed God saying to us: "I want to use you in a significant way. Well, maybe it is time for you to start in that new direction. I have some wonderful opportunities that I want to make available to you. So, if you will just look in my direction I will use you." The problem is that too many of us won't stop long enough to listen or hear what God has to say to us.

As you look forward toward tomorrow, with all of its hidden possibilities, maybe you need to create a new prayer in your mind, a prayer like this one: "God, here I am. Use me! Lead me! If you have something significant planned for my life, count me in. I will follow you the best way that I can. I may be trembling as I say this, but I will trust you will be with me, anywhere and everywhere - always."

Could you pray that prayer. I wonder. How big a dream are you willing to handle? I hope that your eyes are open wide enough so that you might capture the dream that God has in mind for you to accomplish, and that you will work to accomplish it.

SIXTY FOUR

The Importance Of Endurance

I referred before to the comments that Winston Churchill made to the Graduating Class of a Boy's School in Great Britain: "Never Give Up! Never Give Up! Never Give Up!" I was reminded this morning of Leo Tolstoy's statement in his classic work "War And Peace:" "A man on a thousand mile walk has to . . . say to himself every morning. Today I'm going to cover twenty five miles and then rest up and sleep."

Dr. David Jeremiah tells ns "While we shouldn't face each day with grim determination, we need something to carry us. Life requires a sustained determination to remain strong and faithful - step by step, day by day and moment by moment." He refers us to these words in the Petrine Epistle: Dear friends, don't be surprised at the fiery trails you are going through, as if something strange were happening to you (I Peter 4:12 NLT). The point is, you cannot give up, in your life's journey; - not for one moment.

Many a disciple has said that we need our trials and tribulations to prepare us to engage with every situation in our lives: that it is our trying moments that help us to grow. Jeremiah suggests that "only eternity will reveal the purposes of some of our pain."

He reminds us of these words of Harriet Beecher Stowe: "When you get into a tight place, and everything goes against you till it seems as though you couldn't hang on a minute longer, never give up then, for that's just the place and time that the tide will turn." Some one describes this attitude as "having grit." (Angela Duckworth)

She says that to have grit is to hold fast to an interesting and purposeful goal: to invest day after week after year, in challenging practice: to fall down seven times and rise eight."

Think back over your life's walk? How many times did you find yourself facing what seemed to be an impenetrable wall? How often did we finally get through it to the other side? Now we look back and wonder why we had come to that conclusion because now, standing on the other side, we realize that we were adequate to the challenge.

We can think of Churchill telling the people of his war torn country to hold on: that they could win the victory and the war. And they did! And so can YOU!

SIXTY FIVE

The Importance Of Stories

I came across this interesting thought the other day. "It's often the stories that we encounter that change our hearts and motivate our actions!"

Jesus was a master story teller. Somewhere I read someone who suggested that when he was asked a question and responded with a story, that he saw something in the environment or in the background of a situation that triggered his response. We remember all of his stories and the lessons that they taught..

Sadly, the Apostle Paul didn't tell stories. His lessons, though theological, did not excite one's imagination and, therefore, don't come to mind without explanation.

The Preacher who I listen to, each Sunday morning, does not often tell stories. As a result we don't go home with a simple message stapled to our minds. He did tell one today, and it is an important one for all of us.

He is preaching a series of sermons on the song, "Jesus Loves Me!" He was covering the phrase "Little Ones To Him Belong, THEY ARE WEAK BUT HE IS STRONG."

He referred us to the Old Testament Book of Judges, to the story of Gideon. (Judges 7) You will remember the story. The Hebrews were in trouble with the tribe of Midian. The Lord came to Gideon and told him, "Go, with all of your great strength and rescue Israel from the Midianites. I myself am sending you."

On the night before the big battle, the Lord came to Gideon to say: "The men you have are to many for me to give them victory over the Midianites. They might think that they had won by themselves and so give me no credit." Via God's instruction's Gideon's army shrunk from thirty two thousand to twenty thousand.

At that point, God announced "that he still had too many men." So God winnowed down the size of Gideon's Army to three hundred men, "who kept all the supplies and trumpets." The Mideanite Army numbered one hundred thirty five thousand. And we read: "So Midean was defeated by the Israelites and was no longer a threat. The land was at peace for forty years, until Gideon died."

"THEY ARE WEAK BUT HE IS STRONG." The message: Who is on our side." God is!" What else do we need to know about life? "Nothing!" All we need to know is that we are not alone. He is with us, all the way. Don't you ever forget it!

An added thought: What stories might you have to tell that would have meaning and purpose to other people?

SIXTY SIX

On Handling The Unexpected!

Several years ago, while doing research for a sermon, I came across this pregnant paraphrase for several verses in the Epistle of James: "Dear Brothers/Sisters. Is your life full of difficulties and temptations? Then - be happy - for when the way is rough your patience has a chance to grow. So, let it grow, and don't try to squirm out of your problems. For when your patience is finally in full bloom, then you will be ready for anything, strong in character, full and complete." (1:2-4)

The suggestion seems to be, we should be using our moments of testing and temptation as a time to train ourselves for the future and all it holds in store for us.

Needless to say, these quitting points are everywhere. They will be found and experienced in the midst of almost everything we do. We find ourselves thinking about cashing in our chips and moving in some other direction, but the point is we have a choice. These "quitting points" are there to test God's Word and his faithfulness. The proper response might be, to say: "Lord, I am going to stay on my course through this point in my life, trusting that you will get me through this point in my life, and enable me to come out in one piece on the other side."

I read of one clergyperson who offered up this answer: "What we do in the crisis times determines whether we live or slowly die, grow or atrophy, mature or regress back into a state of childlikeness. What we do effects who we are and where we are going."

A woman returned from a Doctor's appointment, where she learned she had a terminal cancer. "Oh," she said to a friend. "I wish I had never been made." Her friend, after thinking for a moment, said rather silently to her, "Helen, you have not been made! You are being made. - NOW!"

I wonder? Is God permitting things to happen to us in order to strengthen and to solidify the genuineness and durability of our commitment? Maybe! What we learn on the mountainpeaks in our life cannot be matched by what we learn down in its valleys.

Martin Buber is a famed Old Testament Scholar. He is commenting on that wonderful scene in the Book of the Exodus when Moses asked God, "What is your name?" And God answers him, "I am who I am!" After studying the Hebrew text for many years, Buber said that he came to the conclusion that we have mistranslated that verse. That is, instead of being translated, "I am Who I Am," Buber said he believed it should read, "I shall be there!" Isn't that a beautiful thought. The name of God is "I shall be there!"

And Jesus said, "I am with you even unto the end of the world!"

When something happens in your life, unexpectedly, guess who is standing next to you? "I Am Who I Am!" He is there! Wow!

SIXTY SEVEN

So Little Time; So Much To Do!

I have a friend who has a favorite sweatshirt that reads "So Many Books; So Little Time." The emphasis is on the number of books available to be read.. I want to reverse those phrases, to put the emphasis on the amount of time we have compared to the number of things we have to do. "To little time. So much we have to do!:"

We hear so much about time management these days. The number of books published in this area is almost overwhelming. "Who has time to read them all? The point that is too often forgotten is that "the value of time depends upon its use." Now many of us have laid the experience of talking to someone who is forever looking at their watch - a not so subtle reminder that they have more important things to do than talk to us.

The Old Testament book of I Kings contains the story of the battle between the defeated King of Syria, Benhadad, and the victorious King of Israel, Ahab. Some weeks after the battle, an unnamed prophet appeared in Ahab's Court with a warning for the Israeli King. It came in the form of a parable. (II Kings 20) It seems that a prisoner of war had been given him to guard, at the cost of a stiff fine or the cost of his life. The prophet said, "but, while your servant was busy here and then, the prisoner was gone."

How descriptive are those words of situations in our own lives. We all know of life's distractions? Steven Covey wrote a book which he entitled, "First Things First," in which he points our attention at life's distractions.

The person who is busy here and there, hasn't thought out what are the most important elements of living. So too, for many of us, the problem persists today. For many of us, today, the world is a gigantic supermarket, with its shelves loaded with necessities and enticing packaged luxuries. How many people do you know to whom life seems so short that they have to rush down the aisles of their years cramming into the basket of their life a thoughtless grabbing of material necessities, sensational indulgences, and ephemeral pleasures? And at the closeout counter, the cost is high. "And while your servant was busy here and there, he was gone: the prisoner escaped!" The guard was spending too much time doing the wrong things, too involved doing the wrong things, too involved in the activity of being busy.

An older, but very successful investor, having learned he cannot focus on too many things at once advises us to make a list of the top twenty five things you want to accomplish in the next few years. From that list, pick the live that are most important to you. Now you have two lists. The investor says, "You avoid at all cost" the longer one, for those items may well prevent the big things from happening.

Dr. David Jeremiah suggests that to move forward in life, we have to discover the beauty of the word no. The practice of a graceful no takes courage, but boy, is it liberating."

Martiza Manress notes in her book, "How To Say No When You Usually Say Yes," "It's alright to say no to lesser things to have room for the best things. Most, of us say yes more than we should because we were taught to be available or because we don't want to damage a relationship. As a result, we're constantly overcommitted, and the greater things are left behind." Remember Andy Stanley's question, "Is it the wise thing to do?"

I don't know how old you are, or how long you have to live, but maybe you need to stop, make a short "Bucket List," and get on moving forward to a successful life. Stop now, for some minutes, and make a list . . and begin work on it!

SIXTY EIGHT
The Responsibility Of Growing Older

I was reading somewhere of some provocative quotations from the pen of Robert Louis Stevenson, when I came upon this thought, "The world is full of a number of things: of so many opportunities." It reminded me of the fact that many of us let our minds sink into one narrow groove or another. We become so preoccupied with petty things that we do not cultivate any new interests. As a result, our lives grow weary; cramped and drab.

I live in a Senior living community and I see and hear those thoughts all around me. For some reason I thought of the Old Testament character we know as Methusaleh. Remember him? We read about him briefly, in Geneses, chapter 5: "When Enoch was 65, he had a son, Methuselah. . . . When Methuselah was 187, he had a son, Lemech, and then lived another 782 years. He had other children, and died at the age of 969." 969 years! Wow! And all he had to show for it was a number of kids. And evidently no one of them amounted to much.

As I look around our community I see any number of individuals who have performed some significant accomplishments. It reminds us that broadening one's interests is not primarily dependent upon having more or less time than anybody else. Rather, it is a matter of being alert and alive and inquisitive.

But here is Methuselah. "He lived 969 years and he died." His life had length, but it lacked what some would call "depth." Put that thought against this one: Take a shallow lake or well. No matter how long or wide or deep it is, it will eventually stagnate, for it needs the depth of new, inflowing water to keep it vital. Think of the Dead Sea. Yet, any person who sees a mountain, - they will want to see it again. It seems that there is an instinct in us, humans, that needs to reach down to great convictions and to reach up to great hopes and desires. Seen any mountains lately? Want to see another one?

One night, an astronomer pointed out a cluster of stars called "Hercules." You can see it with the naked eye. It contains 35,000 stars as bright as our sun: some over one hundred times brighter. The diameter of the cluster is three hundred fifty light years, and it is 36,000 light years away. Now remember that a light year is the distance it takes a ray of light, traveling 186,000 miles per second a year, to cover. Our galaxy, for example, is 300,000 light years in diameter. And there are other such galaxies and spiral nebulae. Astronomers tell us that some of them are are over 170,000,000 light years from us, and that still does not exhaust space. This is to say, when we think of space, we must think in terms of infinity, and we must think of God in the same manner.

Let me suggest that we can attain excellence in the sight of God ONLY if we set our sight on infinity. For a life may be great without any length. It may still be significant, even if it doesn't have the chance to broaden much. But it cannot be a true life unless it has height/depth.

Now, for a moment, think of Jesus of Nazareth. He lived, so we are told, thirty three years. Just thirty three years! But he began each day with a prayer, seeking the peace and strength which passes all our understanding. The results of his life are portrayed before us in his words of insight and hope; his many life changing miracles; his self discipline that awakens in us the desire to keep moving on, in the face of life's turmoils and discouragements. He kept moving on, and accomplished so much. In just thirty three years. Wow!

Why not keep a journal tomorrow; all of the next week? Every day, write down all the words you spoke of encouragement and hope; everyone of the acts of kindness and support you offered. Hopefully, you will be surprised at what you have done. Do more!

I came upon this statement the other day. "Happiness will come to me unexpectedly as a by-product, a surprising bonus for something I have invested myself in."

How we live our life will provide us consequences, both good and bad, for what we do. Give it all the effort you can.

SIXTY NINE

How Fortunate Have You Been In Your Life?

Sometimes I think we need to be reminded about how good life has been to us. Too often we get bogged down by life's negativities and forget about all the good times and unique events that have become a part of our personal history and the blessings that we have been able to enjoy."

I came across a number of words that reawakened those thoughts in my mind. They said: God is extravagant! Unreasonably! Unpredictably! Sometimes, even grotesquely unextravagant. All too often he does so in ways that just don't meet the eye and always in ways that we do not expect or anticipate. But always, in the end, we receive more than we bargained for...

The Psalmist writes: "My cup runneth over." And so it sometimes does. We are trapped in a world and snowed under by his gifts. Our nations bounty hangs heavy on our hands, and our own national heritage, so often described as a godly thing, sits in judgement upon us.

Lets face it, gratitude is the life blood of our faith. It is, in fact, our only resource in the face of God's devastating generosity. We need to remember that in our "pick and choose world" we cannot decide, by ourselves, what to be thankful for.

I remember a story retold by Dr. Reuben Youngdahl about a man named Clarence. He had six children, but with a job that paid hardly enough to keep him more than one step ahead of the sheriff. It was "touch and go," as far as paying his bills was concerned. One day he discovered that the shoes of three of his children were badly worn. He grumbled about having to go out and buy three pairs of shoes, in one strike. As things usually happen in such a home, one emergency followed on the heels of another. The family washing machine managed to break down at about the same time. He couldn't afford a new one, so he scanned the newspaper ads. Spotting a second hand machine, offered for sale, cheap, he went at once to the house listed in the ad. It was a beautiful home. Invited into the kitchen, he saw the latest mechanical equipment: a modern refrigerator, an electric dishwasher, and all the other gadgets which he had read about or seen in the Sears Roebuck Catalogue.

He inwardly commented to himself, "Why couldn't I have things like these at home" - but made the bargain, and arranged to go back the next day to pick up the wash machine. In the conversation with the parents, in the home, he chanced to say, "I've had the toughest breaks. Why just today I had to buy three pairs of shoes for my kids. He wondered then why the woman left the room, leaving the father standing there with tears in his eyes.. "Man," he said, "How fortunate you are. We have only one child, and he has been paralyzed since birth. He has never walked a step. I have never had to buy him any shoes. A much chastened Clarence said later, "I left that house without saying another word and when I got home; first I picked up one of the kids shoes. Sure, the toe was worn because he used them as a brake for his wagon. Then I picked up my daughter's shoes, with holes in the souls, made from skipping rope." Then he picked up another son's shoes, dreadfully out of shape, and still soggy and wet, from his jumping in a puddle, on his way home from school. "That little kid of mine," I thought, "must jump in every puddle he sees on his way home from school." Then, I got down on my knees and thanked God that I had three badly worn pairs of shoes in my house."

Get the message? Never forget it!

SEVENTY

A Must Say Prayer For Everyone Of Us

I recently read the story of Lillian Thrasher. Lillian was working in an orphanage in North Carolina. She felt she had received a "Call from God" to become a missionary in Egypt. She determined to accept the Call, and booked passage to that country. She only had about one hundred dollars in her possession.

One day she was asked to go to the bedside of a dying woman who begged her to care for her malnourished baby girl. Thrasher agreed and the very first orphanage in Egypt had its beginning.

They were to prove to be difficult years, with limited support, but she held on to realize her desire. By the time she died in 1962, Lillian Thrasher had cared for more than eight thousand orphans and had touched many others. This orphanage continues to care for the needy today.

I share the store to introduce you to a prayer that Lillian Thrasher offered when she was very, very young. "Lord, I want to be your little girl. If I can ever do anything for you, just let me know and I'll do it!"

I don't know how old you may be, or where you are, but that is a prayer you need to offer every morning and every evening: **"Lord, if ever I can do anything for you, You just let me know and I will do it!"** And as you offer it, remember, - there are no small tasks in the Lord's work. Nothing you endeavor to do will be time or work wasted.

SEVENTY ONE
We Need To Have A Living God!

I have only met one person who have actually told me that they do not believe in god: in any god!"

People have told me "that they have met people who have said, 'they do not believe in God!'" They said that they have met people who have made that statement, and then asked those same people to describe the god they do not believe in. When those people describe their understanding of God, they respond, "Well I don't believe in that kind of god, either," and the conversation usually ends there.

No, what I mean to say is that I have only met one person who has told me, "they do not believe in God; in any kind of god!"

I was reminded of the youngster who came home from Church School one morning and said to their parents, "Hey, we don't believe in God, do we?" The father responded, "Of course not!" There was a pause, and then the youngster said, "Does God know we don't believe in Him?"

There are many people who will never believe in God until they are confronted by their own weakness and inadequacy. I know people like that, and so do you. That is, as long as we believe we can handle life by ourselves, who needs God?

But when they do need Him! Faith often comes hard and sometimes the only way it comes to us is when we are willing to admit to ourselves, and others, that we cannot go it alone in life. And when we reach that point, then what? Well, you begin to accept him as he is, or at least as you know him to be, and then you endeavor to grow that understanding. Faith, you see, never becomes real, until it becomes personal. That is why, when it comes to a real faith, too many people are on the outside looking in! Remember the father who met Jesus one day and said to him, "Lord, I have faith, but I need more."

In 1859, the tight roap walker, Blondin performed the dangerous feat of crossing Niagara Falls. He performed the act many times and on one occasion carried a bag of sand across it in a wheelbarrow. After the completion of that stunt he asked one of the specastors who had watched him. "Do you think I can carry a man across Niagara, in this wheelbarrow ? The man responded, "Yes, I do!" Then Blondin asked him, "Will you be that man?" "No, I won't!" The real test of faith is not that we say, "We believe!" It is in our willingness to act on what we say we believe.

The young woman was ready to join a Church as a member. She had been living in the community for a long time. She now was pregnant and seemed to have a new perspective on life. When asked why she was ready to become a member of the Church, she said: "I guess it is about time for me to start acting like an adult!

Perhaps it is time for you to grow up to the realization of what the Christian life is really all about. Is it time for you to say, "Lord, I have faith. Help me to have more?"

SEVENTY TWO

How To Handle The Unexpected

I remember reading the story of a doctor, in our country's colonial times, who, while performing an operation, asked his apprentice to administer the anesthetic, which he did. The surgeon asked, "Is he ready?" "He is ready," came back the reply. So, the doctor made his initial incision, but as he did so, the patient screamed out in pain. With disgust in his voice, the physician looked at his assistant and said, "Don't you know how to administer either? Give him some more." The young apprentice did as he was told, but when the doctor touched the patient a second time, with his surgical instrument, again the man on the table grimaced and writhed in pain. "Young man," the doctor said, now very angry, "Young man, don't you know how to administer anesthetic? You are supposed to test the patient." The assistant, already bewildered, said, with some embarrassment: "But sir, I have tested the patient. I have pushed his eye and it doesn't have any reflex: the man ought to be anesthetized." At that moment, the surgeon paused. His face took upon itself its own aura of embarrassment. Then he said: "Oh, I forgot to tell you, he has a glass eye." An unplanned surprise! An unexpected situation!

Which is to say, - in every chapter of our lives, we are likely to come upon an unexpected paragraph or two. There will be a surprise or two that will lift up our spirits and enable us to cruise along on the wheels of some anticipated moments of pleasure and happiness - but there will also be some unexpected roadblocks or tragedies that will push our nose or chin to the ground.

Someone has reflected, "We are pilgrim people! We are pioneers! We are walking through rough snows, high winds, and on difficult roads. We are not living securely settled in comfortable houses. We can expect surprises! Upsets! Upsets! Whatever! But God has given us the wherewithal, through Jesus Christ, to bind these events into the artistry of the total mosaic of life." In the midst of change, in the middle of one upsetting situation or another, we can see God's disclosure of new goals and new personal qualities - if we will just look a little harder.

That being said, with this new insight, we will be able to see our broken dreams redeemed and some higher aspirations born. We don't test God's love by the circumstances in which we find ourselves, rather we can use God's love to interpret the meaning of those situations. We should know that God will never leave us alone, nor will he forsake us. Even when we slip and fall, he will help us to get up and walk, limp, or even hobble along the road of life. But always; always - no matter what or where or when - we need to know this: that we are never walking alone. We need to look away from ourselves and our immediate circumstances - then we will see him. We will see him and know that we are and never will be alone - ever!

SEVENTY THREE
God Has The Final Word!

David wrote down a mouthful of words when he put these words, of Psalm Thirteen on parchment: "How much longer will you forget me, Lord? How much longer will you hide yourself from me?"

How many of us have spoken or felt like speaking these words, ourselves? Well we remember these words of Jesus, spoken from the cross: "My God, My God, Why have you forsaken me?" One of the early Church fathers called this "The dark night of His soul!" It is a common experience.

Sadly, the Bible does not seem to answer this problem or solve the mystery of evil. Rather, it seems to expect the fact that suffering and pain will drop a curtain between humanity and God, so that people will feel that God is absent from their presence.

Commentators, one and all, remind us that David knew that God could be trusted: that there were many things that he did not know and many mysteries that he did not understand, but one thing he did know, - that "God could be trusted."

It is said that when Robert Louis Stevenson was a little boy, he locked himself, one day, in a closet. He panicked and began to scream. His father heard his cries and tried to open the door, but the lock was jammed. A locksmith was sent for, but during the wait, his father kept talking quietly to his son. He calmed his son down and enabled him to maintain his courage. It was this experience that remained as a fixture in Stevenson's mind, when oft-times he thought about his fellowship with his heavenly father. He seemed, in those times, to hear the comforting voice of his heavenly father.

The lesson appears to be, at least in my mind, that tho we will often find ourselves locked in darkness, God will always have the last word, if we will listen to him. He is the keeper of the door that no man can shut.

So, what is God's word, that is available to us when we find ourselves in one of the darker moments in our life? It is a stubborn and unyielding faith in the God of steadfast love. It is a word that I need to hear, though many times I make so much noise that I cannot hear it.

We need to make these words our own: "I will always trust in you, and in your mercy, Lord, and shall rejoice in your salvation." It is a song we need to sing, because he has blessed us so richly.

"Pitch!"

SEVENTY FOUR
It is life's inevitable Question?

I had just opened a new book I had purchased by Louie Giglio. It is not a new book by any means; it was published in 2003. It was just a new book for me: It had been hidden I guess, on the shelf of a Barnes & Noble Bookstore: I just found it there on my last visit.

Giglio's suggestion was that it was a discussion about what we were born to do: all of us. We were all born to worship "Something." Not God, necessarily but something. Early in the book he mentioned Michael Jackson. It was a reminder that those who promote the worship of God had better do a "better job."

Anyway, I came across this statement: ". . eventually we are all captivated by the question of why we are here. Is there a reason for our lives? Is there something we are uniquely destined to do?" I have posed the question to myself and probably to you, as well. "It is the age old question - what's the purpose of life?"

I know the religious answer. But there are a host of people about who are not religious. And although I, personally, don't think there is any other correct answer, many people do. So what is the answer?

Well, that is for you to decide. I think I know.

As far as Giglio is concerned, and that is what his book "The Air I Breathe" is all about, - "You and I exist for one purpose alone - to reflect hack to God his matchless glory. You were made for a unique relationship with him.. And your tile was designed to be a mirror that reflects all the best things about him to the world around you, finding our maker and connecting with his purposes is the one thing we are all seeking."

If you think you have a better answer to life's question, think it through and write it down. If not, you maybe ought to search out Gigilio's book, and work on his answer.

Hopefully, you are going to live a long time: if you are going to live a contented life, and a happy one, as well, it would be wise for you to decide "why you are here?"

Giglio looked around him at the people around him, and asked: "All these people: Do they know their lives have an amazing purpose?

Do you?

SEVENTY FIVE
Help Is Here!

In this hurry/scurry pandemic/post pandemic world of ours, we all need to bear a word of hope! The Texas pastor Max Lucado offers us a whole book of hope in his writing "Help is Here!" In one of the early chapters, he shares this thought.

"A friend tells me about the day his ten year old son ran away from home. After being gone the entire day, the boy walked tip the driveway with his head hung low. "Son," the father asked, "what did you learn today?" The boy answered, "I learned that everywhere I go, I go with me." Don't we all."

Lucado goes on to say: "We take our greed, our selfishness, our wounds and warts" with us. "We dare not think for a moment that we have the power to be the persons God wants us to be. But nor do we dare to think that God will fail to give it to us. He empowers us to be what God calls us to be. This was the promise Jesus made to a certain religious leader who paid him a late night visit."

Thankfully, the boy's father or someone else had taught the young lad to think through his intentions.

On another occasion, I went to the front door of our home to find a distraught father standing before me. He had just found his son, in a spot behind a nearby Elementary school, dead, from a self inflicted gun shot wound. He had been faced with a personal act that he thought was going to do significant damage to his plans for his life. We had failed to teach the young boy, ready to graduate from High School, to think through his situation and discuss his problem with us.

Similar situations; drasticly different outcomes! Remember the QUESTION: "Is this the wise thing to do?" It keeps coming up before us, doesn't it?

But back to the religious leader I spoke about a few paragraphs ago. It was Nicodemus. And the incident is in John, chapter 3.

He had come to Jesus, in the late night hour, to talk to him, under (he cover of darkness: Lucado notes, and I had not noted this before, Nicodemus did not ask Jesus a question, but Jesus answered the query that was evidently bewildering him, "Truly, truly I say to you, unless one is born again, be cannot see the kingdom of God."

What Jesus was saying, Lucado suggests was, "If you want to get the best out of life, and this would be to live God's way, "You must be born again," or, in other words, "Go back to the beginning and start over."

As far as Nicodemus was concerned, what a person can and cannot do, is all about human effort, human gumption, human achievement. In his view, the gate to heaven was greased with elbow grease."

"Jesus, on the other hand, made reference to our human inability: to what humans can do without God's help." We all know the story. It is the classic conversation. Man on the one hand. God on the other. Whose side should we be on? Friend, there is only one answer. Period!

The last Norman Vincent Peale, when asked how people should deal with their difficult situations, suggested that we make two lists. What you can do to face them by yourself and what you can do to face them if God is at your side?

When you do your lists, there is no comparison. "With God on your side" win's very time.

Take out a fresh piece of paper. What situations are confronting you today? What can you do about them? What could you do about them with God's help? Make your lists! Say your prayers! What is your answer?

Jesus said, "You must be born again," meaning, "Maybe it is time to rethink where you are and whose you are" before you go any further in life. "Go back to the beginning and start over again." "Yes, and with the awareness that God is at our side, let us face our situations with a new mind, aware that God is ready to walk with us through the situations that life presents to us.

Is it time for you to be born again, and to start living your life in a new, God honoring way?

SEVENTY SIX

The Importance Of Living A Pro-Active Life!

Many of us have lived through what I would call "The Steven Covey years." We were told about living "Re-active and Pro-active lives."

I thought about Covey when I read these words of Dr. David Jeremiah, in his book "Forward:" "Don't minimize the opportunities God has set for your future. Don't put all your efforts into avoiding loss or turn your face away from the future. He has planned for you. Instead go forward with confidence and courage to do the task he has set for you."

Those words reminded of these words that Nehemiah spoke to God from Jerusalem: ". . (remember) you did not abandon them there in the desert (during the Exodus), for your mercy is great. You did not take away the cloud or the fire that showed them the path by day and night." (Nehemiah 9:19) And these words of the prophet Ezekiel: "I will put my spirit in you and you will see to it that you follow my laws and keep all the commands I have given you.." (Ezekiel 36:27)

Dr. Jeremiah asks us, in the midst of our Exodus: "What is your Cannan? What does God want you to tackle, to accomplish for him?" "If you risk nothing, then you risk everything."

Then he quotes another who said, "If you can get excited about the future, the past won't matter. . . Even when the world is coming apart at the seams; when global panics and pandemics are the order of the day; when our economy is uncertain and our faith is under assault; even then - especially then - you need to look ahead to the next step God has for you."

"Several years ago, a Florida Newspaper profiled seventy one year old designer Lileth Hogarth. She grew up watching her mother sew clothes for her family in Jamaica, and Lileth has kept people in stitches ever since - literally. She once said: "You're never dead until you're dead. . . And you should keep your dream alive as long as you are alive."

In a paraphrase of Romans 12:2, Paul writes: "Don't copy the behavior and customs of this world, but let God transform you into a new person, by changing the way you think. Then you will learn to know God's will for you, which is good and pleasing and perfect." Remember the Proverb: "Trust in the Lord with all your heart, and lean not on your own understanding. He is completely able to lead you where he wants you to go." (Prov. 3:5)

Dr. Jeremiah writes: "Do you ever end the day or the year, asking your self, What was all that for? What did I accomplish? What difference did I truly make? When you find your purpose, you stop chasing things that will never satisfy you. Instead you find the joy of pursuing the next steps God has for you."

In the unmined chapters if his book, "Forward", Dr. Jeremiah notes these words of Billy Graham's daughter Ann Graham Lotz: "I just try to faithfully follow the Lord step by step, and day by day. Ten years from now, I just want to look back . . and know that to the best of my ability, I have been obedient to God's call on my life."

As one wise man put it: "We are not to read the Bible just for curiosity or intellectual reasons alone. We're to study it to discover God's will for (the rest of our lives.) We read it to heed it!

Do you have a plan for the rest of your life? Not a "Bucket list!" But a plan for the next stage of your life: for your pre-retirement, your retirement; your post retirement. Make one while you still have some time. You will be the better for it. Everyone will the better for it.

Do it! Now!

SEVENTY SEVEN

Guess Who Came/Is Coming To Dinner?

GOD! He was there! Will be there! Did you miss him?

I think it was in Junior High when I saw the movie; the story of a cobbler who had a dream; maybe it was a vision? One night he heard what he thought was the voice of God, and it said "I am going to visit you tomorrow!"

The next morning he arrived at his place of business and went to work cleaning it up, He straightened all of the shoes in their place. He even washed the windows, swept the floor; watered the plants. And he waited and waited and waited. It turned out to be a very slow day. He seemed to spend an inordinate amount of time looking out the window.

As he watched the street he spied a young lad, evidently alone, standing in the shade of a doorway across the street. He looked tired and weary and alone. "Hey, young man," he cried as the boy seemed ready to run. . "Come over here, and let me share my lunch with you." It was a refreshing time for both of them. They talked, ate, and then the boy went on his way; refreshed, and the cobbler went back to his waiting. "When will he come," he wondered.

He decided he had to get some work done, so he went to his bench and almost absently minded went to work on a pair of shoes. The door opened. He was almost afraid to look up. "Was it him?" o, it was an elderly woman, who appeared to be exhausted by the heat. Oh, she was thirsty. "Would he give her some water?" "Certainly!" She sat down, rested, drank; was refreshed. "Thank you!" And she was on her way. But still, he didn't come. He waited and waited and then waited some more.

Quitting time was fast approaching and still there was no sign of his expected visitor. He began to close up his shop. There was a sadness in his shuffle and a tear in his eyes. Had he misunderstood? Maybe it had been only a dream? He stepped out onto the walk and put his key in the lock. Then, he turned around and slowly walked home.

All during the preparation of his evening dinner he wondered, "Why had he not come?" He cleaned the table and washed the dishes and was about to sit down, when there was a knock at the door. It was an old man, disheveled, dirty; his clothes were tattered and torn. He had not eaten all day. He was alone. "Might there be a place where he could spend the night?" "No," at least not here. There was shrugging of the shoulders. The man turned and began to walk away. "Wait! I do have a room!" The room where he and his wife had slept. He has not been able to use it since she had died. And he had some clothes and some food left over from supper. Then it was time to sleep. He bid his guest good night, and went to his own room, undressed in the evening light, and wondered again, "Why had he not come, as he said he would?"

He put on his night clothes, washed his hands and face, brushed his teeth, and prepared to go to bed. Then he noticed the book, lying there on a side table. He picked it up and began to read, at random, from the page before him. "When the Son of man comes as a king, and all the angels with him, he will sit on his royal throne, and the people of all of the nations will be gathered before him. Then he will divide them into two groups; just as the shepherd separates the sheep from the goats. He will put the righteous people on his left and the others on his left. Then the king will say to the people on his right, 'Come, you that are blessed by my father. Come and possess the kingdom which has been prepared for you, ever since the foundation of the world, I was hungry and you fed me, thirsty and you gave me drink. I was a stranger and you received me into your home; naked and you clothed me.' The righteous will then answer him, "When Lord, did we ever see you hungry, and feed you or thirsty and give you drink or naked and clothe you? When did we ever see you sick or in prison, and visit you?" The king will then reply, "I tell you, whenever you did this for one of the least of these brothers of mine, you did it for me!"

And suddenly it dawned upon the cobbler.. He "had" come. He "had" kept his word. And the cobbler then realized he had almost missed him, because he had not been looking for him as he was. He had been looking for someone he had created in his mind's eye; for one who was greater than life; for one who was about and apart from it all, and he had almost missed him.

How often have you missed him in the day to day living of your life?

Don't miss him again!

SEVENTY EIGHT

The World Needs More Optimists!

The first Service Club that I joined was the Optimists. Then, as now, its Mission Statement read: "To provide hope and positive vision. Optimists bring out the best in kids." An optimist seeks to bring out the best in themselves and others! Jesus Christ was a great proponent of optimism.

A Christian Pharisee by the name of Paul wrote these words, "I can do all things through Christ who strengthens me." (Philippians 4:13) His writings are filled with words of Optimism. The Presbyterian pastor. John Henry Jowett, wrote of him, "His eyes are always illumined. The cheery tone is never absent from his speech. The buoyant and springy movement of his life never changed. The light never dies out of his sky . . The apostle is an optimist."

Dr. David Jeremiah shared these words, after reading the words in Romans 15:13, "Now may the God of hope fill you with all joy and peace, believing that you may abound in hope by the power of the Holy Spirit:" Then he adds, "May I suggest that you pray those words every morning, every noontime, and every evening until you know them by heart. That prayer can adjust your mindset in any given season of life, deepen your core convictions, and strengthen your belief. ."

In the fortieth year of his life, away back in 1967, the Actor/Comedian Dick Van Dyke, was in a Doctors office, and having been informed that he was going to have to deal with the problem of arthritis, as his life progressed, and that he would be using a walker, if not a wheelchair within five years, did something very rash. Suddenly, being seared, he stood up in the examining room and starting tapping his toes, then shuffling around, then dancing, "as if proving to himself he could still order his body, to do a soft shoe, anytime he wanted." He said "I was forty years old. And I have not stopped moving ever since. Nor do I plan to hit the stop moving button any time soon . . . As a card carrying 'the glass-is-half-full optimist' I'm going to . . declare that old age doesn't have to be a dreary weather report. In 99.9 percent of the stories I have heard, it is better than the alternative, if only because you get to see what happens next. How can you not be curious?"

Dr. H. Norman Wright notes: Depending on how active your mind is, you may produce more than 45,000 thoughts a day. . . It might be compared to a flock of birds flying in and out of your mind." Dr. Jeremiah, a much deeper thinker than I am, instructs us: "Learn to talk to yourself instead of listening to your self. Learn to preach to yourself. Learn to encourage yourself in the Lord. It will change the way you speak to others. Your mood and message will be different, even in the midst of difficulties."

The world needs more optimists, and you and I could be one of them!

These words were presented to me in a Prayer Of Confession on Sunday morning: "We confess that are are indifferent to your will. You call us to proclaim your name but we are silent. You call us to do what is just, but we remain idle. You call us to live faithfully, but we are afraid. Give us courage to follow in your way, that joined with those from ages past, who have served you with faith, hope, and love, we may inherit the kingdom . . "All of us, no matter what our faith may be, can offer up those words. They tell us who we are, and about some changes we ought to make.

It was the atheistic philosopher Frederick Nietzsche who said of the Christians he knew: "I would believe in their salvation if they looked like people who have been saved." I think he was saying: "live out what you say you believe." Do you? Probably not. Using that Prayer and the challenge of Mr. Nietzsche, what changes do you need to make in your life?

If you think you can't do something, you probably won't. If, on the other hand, you think you can, odds are you will. The same is true with your problems. If you dwell on them, they will overwhelm you. But if you will look for solutions, you will find some.

Craig Groeschel notes: "What you do today is a result of your thoughts in the past. What you become in the future will reflect what you think about today."

Be an Optimist! Remember: You can be one step closer to changing your thinking and believing what God has to say about you!

SEVENTY NINE

We All Need To Do Our Part

A man tells of taking his car to the garage for some repair work. On his way home, the engine did not seem to be performing as well as it had before he had taken the car in; some two hundred dollars earlier. He returned to the garage, and asked the mechanic to take another look. The owner seemed to think something was missing, and asked the mechanic if he had not noticed that something was missing? "Yes," was the response, but I didn't take it off. Someone else did, and I ain't got time to fix what someone else did!"

Some years ago, a priest retired. He had been a wonderful priest. Everybody loved him. His parish wanted to do something special for him! Now, the people in his northern California parish were mostly grape farmers and wine makers, so they decided to make him a gift of their finest wines. A barrel was set up in the town square, and it was announced that everyone was to bring a jug of their best wine, and add it, to the contents in that receptacle, during the coming week. Then, on Sunday, when the priest performed his final Mass, they had a little ceremony, and presented him with the barrel.

Needless to say, the cleric was touched by their token of affection, and said that he could not possibly enjoy the barrel of wine by himself. He wanted his friends to have some to. So, he called for spigot and glasses. They plunged the spigot into the barrel, and prepared to draw off the first glass of wine. When the handle of the spigot was turned, nothing happened; nothing came out but water. What had happened? Well, every member of the Parish, thinking it would not matter if they gave water instead of wine, instead had left it up to all the others to provide the wine.

I was reminded of the incident in Jesus' ministry, when four friends brought another to Jesus; removed a portion of a buildings roof, and lowered their friend, on a blanket, into Jesus' presence. Four friends! They each had a corner to carry, They all did their job as they saw their friend healed.

Holding up your corner! Really believing that God can help! Believing it enough to take a risk: to become more involved in someone else's life.

A minister tells about a business man in the Church he served. One day he was sitting in a Church School Class, when he heard a member say that he was praying for a friend who needed some help. Later, he heard him pray for his friend: "Lord, please put your loving arms around my friend." following the class session, the minister went up to the "concerned" friend and said, "What's wrong with putting YOUR arms around your friend?" That's how people really feel God's arms around them.

Maybe there is still time for us to hold up our corners! Maybe all we needed was to get the idea that it is "our" responsibility to hold up our corner in life.

Well, now you have heard about it. So get with it! And God be with you!

EIGHTY

Is It Never Too Early Or Too Late To Retire?

In his Book "Finish: Give Yourself The Gift Of Done." Jon Acuff writes: According to studies. 92 percent of New Year's resolutions fail. Every January, people start with hope and hype, believing that this will be the New Year that does indeed deliver a New You. But though 100 percent start, only 8 finish."

Commenting on this observation, Dr. David Jeremiah writes: "But if you don't finish what you start, it's like a building that never has a roof." And then he adds: "The lesson? You're not finished until you're finished. You're not done until your done. Therefore, stay focused all the way through, because it isn't over until its over." It sounds like something dial Yogi Berra might say!

Dr. Jeremiah then notes: "My friend Harry Boilback, still very active in his nineties, says: 'I retire every night to go to bed so that I can get up the next morning to find out what God has for me to do." Sitting on the side of his bed he says: 'God, here's another day. I am glad I'm still here. You must have something for me to do. What I want to do is to magnify Your name. I want to please you in all that I do.'" That's a great bedside prayer, no matter what your age.

One man summarizes his problem in this way: "I feel so lonely and depressed. I miss my job, the office, my lunch buddies and friends at work. I used to be very busy at work, and now suddenly there is nothing to do, no deadlines, etc. So this is what retirement is - boring and lonely. I wish I could be happy again like the good old days."

His wife responded. "What are you planning to do today?" He replied. "Nothing!" "But you did that yesterday." "I know, but I'm not finished yet."

So, the question arises, "What do you plan to do when you retire?" The positive reply is: Remember "Retirement is simply God's way of freeing you up for further service." Dr. Jeremiah's thought was: "I've observed that those who finish best never consider themselves retired from their basic calling from God." The Christian Apostle, Paul of Tarsus, remarked: "The gifts and the calling of God are irrevocable."

In other words, to my way of thinking, you and I still have work to do. Take a look around. You have an idea as to what gifts you received, as you grew up. What is there - out there - that there is a possibility for you accomplish, no matter what your age.

Remember - God can still hear your prayers. Talk to him. That might be all you need to do!

EIGHTY ONE

Sometimes The Only Answer Will Be "No!"

There are some prayers, maybe only one, that God will not answer in your life. No matter how serious the situation may be; no matter how often you pray the prayer, the answer will always be "No!" "No!" "No!"

I never have ever had such a thought but Charles Swindoll, in his book "Clinging To Hope" hit me in the face with that thought. This is what he wrote: "Simply put, it isn't God's will that everyone be healed in this life." He goes on to say: "But the fact is, God never promises that everyone will be physically healed on this side of eternity."

Daniel Krauthammer, the son of the late Columnist Charles Krauthammer, wrote in his father's eulogy - lessons learned from his father. "Don't be defined by what life throws at you and you cannot control. Accept the hand you are dealt with grace, and then go on to play that hand as joyously, industriously and vigorously as you can."

Mr. Swindoll reminds us of some of the words we read in the Epistles. He quotes words, as in the Epistle of James, "Just as God is the source of wisdom to understand hardships (1:5), He's also the source of our strength to endure them." (See Romans 15:5). He points our attention to the Epistle Of Colossians, where the Apostle Paul petitions his readers, "We also pray that your will be strengthened with all glorious power so that you will have all the endurance and patience you need." (1:11)

Swindoll writes to suggest that when we come upon a situation that seems to big for us to handle, that we offer this prayer: "Lord, I am in a mess, part of which I caused and part of which I didn't. It has brought loss, heartache, feelings of failure and disappointment to me and to others. I need you to help me to see through your eyes where I can't see through my own. Help me Lord, to grow through this experience, to look at these troubles from your perspective. By your grace, let me ponder it rightly and gain a proper understanding of it. I desperately need your wisdom because I don't have it within myself..":

Wise man that he is, Swindoll then offers this conclusion: "God knows your circumstances right now. He knows the various troubles you are experiencing - those that come and go and those that come and stay. In fact, when God walked the earth, He endured the same kinds of trials, temptations and sufferings we endure. And because God calls us his children (John 1:12; Romans 8:14), I can assure you that he will faithfully lead you by the hand through your darkest valley." (Psalm 23:4)

Phillip Yancey observes: "We have different roles to play, we and God. As God made clear to Job, we humans lack the capacity to figure out providence and cosmic justice and answers to the "Why?" question."

I think there is only one real answer to the "Why" question: "Why Not?" I really like Charles Krauthammer's words: "Accept the hand you are dealt with grace, and then go on to play that hand joyously, industriously and as vigorously as you can." In other words take what life throws at you and "live with it." with God's help as best you can.

I remember a song: I think it was in the days of World War II: "Praise The Lord And Pass The Ammunition." That's how we can deal with life's unanswered prayers. "Pray for deliverance, always. However, in the meanwhile, and for the rest of your life, ask God to provide you with ways to deal with your situation. You can do that, and I believe he will give you the way to walk with him, through it.

Think of the geography of Psalm 23. In Psalm 22, we find the cry: "My God! My God! Why have you abandoned me?" (22:1) And in Psalm 24, we are blessed with these words of triumphant victory, "The world and all that is in it, belong to the Lord, the earth and all who live on it are his." (Psalm 24:1) And between our troubles and our tomorrow's, as we walk through life's dark places, we walk with The Shepherd. "Even if I go through the deepest darkness, I will not be afraid, Lord, for you are with me." (Psalm 23:4)

Friends! Again the words of Mr. Krauthammer: "Don't be defined by what life throws at you." You are a child of God.

Reach out your hand. He is holding it out for you. There you have it.

EIGHTY TWO
We Are Never Alone!

Many years ago, now, Professor Robert Webber, speaking to a chapel full of students, focused their attention on the Third Commandment. Expanding on what might be called "the narrowness" of the Commandment "Thou Shalt Not Take The Name Of The Lord In Vain," he told his attentive listeners "they should never live as though God does not exist," or, if you state his words positively, "Always live with an awareness of God's existence" - always remember that you are never alone.

When my bride and I were on our Honeymoon in New York City, she said one day, that we could do whatever we wanted to do, because nobody knew us. We were living in a small town; this was New York City. Some hours later, we were in our Hotel Room, when the phone rang. It was one of her High School friends who told us that they had heard we were in the city. So were they! "Could we have lunch together." We are NEVER alone?

We learn from our study of The Hebrew Bible, that our Jewish forefathers had a host of rules reminding them that the land on which they lived was God's property. This is God's world! Human life is sacred. We BELONG to God and we ought never forget it.

The people growing up in America today have long ago forgotten such thoughts. We are told we can do ANYTHING we want to do, whenever we want to do it. I "swear" a lot more than I used to. I am not always aware of God's presence. But he is always there "listening."

Right now: now think about this for a moment: have you been living today: as if God is present? Be honest now! Friends, we are never alone.

The question you need to ask yourself is: how can I remember; always remember, that I am a child of God, and that he is watching me every moment, every day? I don't mean to make you paranoid, just aware of the way life is.

I would guess that there is no one way to accomplish this reality. Everyone has to go at it in their own way. Someone suggests that we might wear a ring or a bracelet, to remind us of God's presence with us. Look at "it" and remember!

Henri Nouwen recommends that we practice "praying without ceasing." That is what the Apostle Paul would have us do. "To pray unceasingly does not mean to think about God in contrast to thinking about other things, or to talk to God instead of talking to other people. Rather, it means to think, speak, and live in the presence of God." He goes on to say: "One way to stand in the presence of God, and pray unceasingly, is to meditate by using the "Jesus Prayer." Remember the lax Collector's prayer, found in The Gospel of Luke: "Lord, have mercy on me, a sinner." That is what the Eastern Orthodox tradition calls it.

Nouwen writes, "Repeating that simple phrase, very slowly, takes on a meditative quality that brings peace and repose to the soul. The words can become part of our breathing; of our whole way of living.." We can take that prayer with us, anywhere and everywhere. And you don't even have to close your eyes when you say it. "Thus we can pray without ceasing!"

Find your own solution, but find one that works for you.

You are never alone! And don't you forget it!

EIGHTY THREE

Are You Comfortable With Your Life/In Your Life?

I came across an interesting book the other day. I saw it advertised in the magazine "Christianity Today." I ordered it got it, and I began to read it. You ought to do that sometime. When you see a book advertised, buy it. It might have a message from God, just for you and, maybe, for somebody else who God will reach through you.

The title of the Book was, "Necessary Christianity" and the author's name is Claude R. Alexander.

He wrote it, thinking about the way he was living his life, believing that he was comfortable with who God called him to be and what God had called him to do." It made me wonder if I felt the same way about my life.? He went on to say, "God calls the Christian, in fact every one, to live with a sense of the necessary; "to live within the will of God and under the voice of God."

He then suggested that the immature person (Christian) views life . . . from the standpoint of options. That too many of us see God's claim on us as one of the many options we can choose: many of us we see much of life as random, accidental and haphazard." "The world says we can negotiate with God. We can strike a compromise with God. We can delay and even deny the call of God and claims of God on us and for us. The dictates of God are a matter of what we might do and not what we must do. They are possibilities, not necessities." We'll do that tomorrow! Sound like you sometimes think?

He then strikes the theme of his book. "God is calling for Christians to grow up to him and realize that he calls us to a life of the necessary. He calls us to realize the 'mustness' of our life with him."

He went on to say: "The mature believer in Christ views his or her life from the standpoint of necessity. We (must) understand we are here because it is necessary that we are here." We are with and for a purpose. "Our life is not optional or elective. Our life is necessary. Our life is essential; is compulsory. There is an indispensable aspect to our being.. We are here because it is necessary that we are here." We have things to do today! "You are here because you must be here. You exist because your existence is necessary for this time in the history of the world." Think of what one missing part can do to a puzzle on your game table?

Alexander suggests: "I must keep the intentionality of my life in focus." Just like the Carpenter from Nazareth had a direction and aim to his life" so - there is a purpose toward which your life is drawn. To paraphrase the words of Jesus: "YOU must be about your father's business."

Alexander's word to you is: "The fact that we are alive and occupying space on earth is because our life is about something. There is intention to our life and for our life." "There's a reason we have the talents, gifts and passions we do. There's also a reason we've had the opportunities we've had."

Listen to more he has to say. "This recognition of the intentionality of life not only tells us that our life is about something, it also informs us that our life should be about something." "Are we about what our life is about?"

I wonder, - hasn't Alexander made you feel important? You should feel important! Is there something out there that you are still to do? I wonder.

EIGHTY FOUR
Can We Start All Over Again?

The story is told about a school bus driver who, on the last day of school before the Spring vacation, issued new school bus passes to his passengers, as they boarded the bus, and asked them to deposit their old, frazzled passes, ones they had been carrying since the start of the school year, in a basket next to his seat. He said: "He wanted them to have new passes for his successor, whom they would meet following the vacation period." He told those who asked him "the why of it all." "He was going to Las Vegas to spend his vacation period. If he won, he was going to retire."

On the first day, following the vacation, that very same bus driver opened the door of the bus in silence and as his young passengers boarded, he checked each new, clean pass, as if he had never seen the student before, and they responded in much the same way.

Here was a man, no matter what his age, who wanted to make a fresh start in his life; perhaps revisit an old dream or create a new one - and who of us has not thought about doing much the same thing, at one time or another in our lives? "If only," we think "could I start over again?"

In one of his plays, the writer John Ervine, has one of his characters say, "To me, the most wonderful thing in the world is not the young man beginning life with ideals; we all do that, but the old man dying with them undiminished."

I guess the question I am asking you is this, "How do YOU make the most of all the arts, that is "the art of living," when no one treats it as an art? Too few of us treat life as an art. I think we ought to. If only I could begin my life all over again.

If I could begin my life again? Let me share some possibilities with you. If I could begin "my life" all over again, I would pray, by the grace of God, to be more of a person: more deep, more human, more humane. Francis Willard, the great woman campaigner, said, when asked "what she would do if she could live her life over again, "I would praise more and blame less."

A man, walking with a friend, who happened to be a Navajo Indian, in Times Square in New York City, during the noon hour. All of a sudden, the Indian stopped and said, "I think I hear a cricket chirping." Right, thought his friend! "You hear a cricket chirping, in Times Square, right now? Heck, I can hardly hear myself think." The Indian walked over to the curb, bent down, and, sure enough, he came up with a cricket in his hand. We see and we hear what we are looking for. **I would hope by the grace of God, to give more love to people: to be more aware of them, and the things that they need in life.**

Friends, thee are people out there - in your community, maybe even next door; in your workplace, who could use a little bit more love in their lives. You could touch them, and make a big difference in their lives.

I would like to spend my life being involved in developing the purposes of God. One man retired and spent his life creating "jigs" so that blind people could be employed in a certain industry. He opened up a whole new world to himself and for others, after he retired. The problem with too many of us is that we are wonderful but undeveloped people.

If you could begin your life all over again, what would that mean to you and for the world around you? Coming home from worship, one morning, we saw this wonderful, thought provoking message on a Church Lawn sign: "Whatever your past has been, your future is spotless!" Wow!

Your future begins today! How will you spend the rest of your life?

EIGHTY FIVE

The Possibilities Of A New Experience!

While reading the book written by Bishop Claude Alexander, which he titled "Necessary Christianity," I came across these words which speak to what I believe are the meaning and purpose behind my intent for the book you are now reading.

These are Alexander's words: "The life of the Christian is fraught with occasions where the crowds say to us, "Stay right here!" He defines our situation in this way. "The temptation is to remain static. It is to localize ourselves within one point in time and space. It is to be satisfied with where we are and who we are, such that we don't move any further forward in life."

He goes on to say: "It hits us on the level of our minds. We are tempted to be satisfied with the current way we think. We are content with our thoughts. We don't need any new ideas. We don't need any new mental challenges. We don't need any different concepts or approaches. After all, we've done pretty well with the approaches and concepts we already have. Why rock the boat? Why mess with a good thing? If it isn't broken, don't fix it."

A bit later, the writer speaks the answer I am writing about. "For the disciple of Jesus Christ, life is not static; it is dynamic. . . It is not one big moment but a series of moments, each proceeding from the other. God is not a static God. He is dynamic." To remember Steven Covey, "he is proactive, not reactive."

"That's why the mature Christian can confidently say, 'The best is yet to come.' (We can look forward to the good old daz!") Whatever God has done in, for, with and through our life is not so we can become self-satisfied and stuck but so we can be strengthened and readied for what is ahead." . . "God seeks to expand his influence by providing us expanded opportunities to be and do today. There are other realms where he wants to be known through us. There are other dimensions where he wants to be seen by us. There are other circles where he wants to be felt through us. There are other spheres where God wants to be strengthened through us."

To repeat the words of Bishop Alexander: "The life of the believer is not about what the believer wants. It's about what God wants for the believer. It's about what God desires for us and from us. It's about the lines that God has drawn for our life. It's about what God has appointed and assigned." . . "God isn't making our life up as we go. God has drawn the lines of our life. He has established the path and terrain of our life. There are certain appointments and assignments God has for our life that we haven't even dreamed or imagined."

We live in a retirement community. Last night, at dinner, I noticed my wife waving at a number of (widowed) women as they came in for their evening meal. These gals live alone, in a one bedroom apartments. They come out for dinner, and then return to their rooms for the rest of the day. That "wave" is an act of friendship that will last them a whole day. She is a "friendly person;" always has been. That is one of the reasons site is here, where we live. She is being used by her God to show his love to his people.

Why are you where you are? Consider your special gifts? How are you using them, no matter how old or young you are?

EIGHTY SIX
Getting Out Of Us What Is In Us!

I remember hearing the story of the angry parishioner who accosted Princeton Seminary professor Norman Victor Hope, to complain about his preacher who "read" his morning pastoral prayer. The professor responded by asking if the same minister preacher used a manuscript in the pulpit? "Yes, he does," was the reply. "Do you think that is alright?" Hope asked. "Yes," said the parishioner, "because it allows him the opportunity to better speak to God for his congregation." Then came this statement: "If the minister uses a prepared message to address his congregation, why is it not important that he use a prepared prayer to speak to God?"

I was reminded of these words of Dr. Hope, as I was making my way through the gathered writings of the late Roman Catholic priest. Henri Nouwen, used to create the book the Editors entitled "Spiritual Direction." Nouwen wrote: "Writing is the process in which we discover ourselves. The writing, itself, reveals to us what is alive in us. The deeper satisfaction of writing is precisely that it opens up new spaces within us of which we were not aware before we started to write. To write is to embark on a journey of which we do not know the final destination." Nouwin wrote: "I do not know what I carry in my heart but I trust that it will emerge as I write," . . And "Once we dare 'to give away' on paper the few thoughts that come to us, we start to discover how much is hidden underneath these thoughts and thus we gradually come in touch with our own riches and resources." The words and thoughts are there, just below the surface of our living, waiting to be discovered and shared with ourselves, and maybe, with those around us.

Over the years I have often heard or read of the importance of expressing ourselves in one exercise or another. As Dr. Hope told that upset parishioner, there is significant value in writing out our prayers: of taking the time to creatively or otherwise, put our prayer thoughts on paper, before we think or speak our prayers. In other words, before we make our personal prayers a reality in our devotional moments, we ought to write them down before we offer them.

Think of the words I noted earlier: I do not know what I carry in my heart, but I trust that it will emerge as I write." In the process, we do not make our prayers, they make us. "Once we dare to give away on paper the few thoughts that come to us, we start to discover how much is hidden underneath these thoughts and thus we come in touch (with ourselves.)"

Further along, in their research, they came across these words of Nouwin: "As we live out "our stories," we will find that "it is in the valleys that we need to remember the mountain top." Sometimes we need to pause, in the midst of our thinking and reading, and let ourselves in on what God is trying to say to us. As we read, Nouwin suggests, we ought to let "the written words enter into our minds and descend into our hearts." As they do we become different people. "The word gradually becomes flesh in us and transform our whole being.

In my growing up days, girls spent a lot of time, "Writing in their diaries." Those writings have sparked a lot of thoughts as their families have read them, often discovering them in an attic box, etc. Those jottings revealed what their ancestor or family member were all about. Today, we are often encouraged to keep a "Journal," - a sophisticated "Diary". Such an endeavor will not only be of value to others, as they later read our words: but they can also be important to us, as we get in touch with ourselves.

Nouwin wrote: "Writing is the process in which we discover ourselves." It might be a hidden value for you to practice. Try it out. Maybe, today you might try "writing out your prayer thoughts!" See if they help you to grow your prayer life.

And maybe, for a week or two, you might try "keeping a Journal." In a week or so, go back over your writings and see what you might learn about yourself.

EIGHTY SEVEN
There Is Always Time To Begin Again

I was reading, devotionally, in the Pauline Epistle to the Philippians, and I was confronted by these famous words m Chapter 3:

"I do not claim that I have already succeeded or have already become perfect. I keep striving to win the prize for which Christ Jesus has already won me to himself. I do not think that I have already won it; the one thing I do, however, is to forget what is behind me and do my best to reach what is ahead." I strain forward to what lies ahead. I press on (I reach! I strain forward - toward the goal!)

In my file I came across some notes I had written from the book "Annapurna." It is the story of a mountain by that name and the work that went into reaching its summit, some 26,493 feet in the air. The story told how climbers plan the assault of a mountain; how the base camps and the successive camps are laid out; and finally of the preparation for assailing the heights. In those high places, the author writes, "the best energy is an enormous problem. The lifting of a fool requires all of a person's concentration. Each person seems isolated in a world of their own. Human flesh, bone, and blood can stand just so much atmospheric pressure." When they were within two hours of the summit, two hours seemed to be an eternity. The leader of the expedition said, to the writer of the book, who was funding the adventure, - in words punctuated with a feeling of agony: "What will you do if I turn back." The reply was, "Then I shall go on alone." "Then I will go with you," said his comrade.

Inch by inch they climbed to a place where only the sky was in front of them.

Though the wind tore at them, with such velocity that they could barely keep their footing, in one ecstatic moment they realized they were standing on the top of the world. The author writes, "It wasn't the view with all of its far flung panorama that elated us. Rather, it was that this high place had a certain clearness, a contact with time and space and God. What filled our hearts with joy, was the deep insight which suddenly burst out of our souls. There, in the midst of our aloneness came the awareness that, within ourselves, there was something indestructible, invulnerable, indomitable. Something which nothing in the world could destroy."

You know, we have within us the enormous capability of being able to rise up against any situation that life may throw our way, and win!

In Colorado Springs, Colorado there is an Institute called "The Olympic Training Center." They train our nation's foremost athletes there, subjecting them to intense rigid scrutiny. They are photographed at 2,000 frames per second; every breath is measured. Coaches count every heartbeat and watch every move, looking for the tiniest flaws, in the hope that they can gain or save as little as one hundredth of a second in performance time. Here are people who are willing to submit to arduous training, to help them reach the mark in the shortest possible length of time. They will strain for it with all of their might.

What our society identifies as the proper intensity for successful athletic achievement, the Apostle Paul associates with our involvement in the Christian life. If there is the smallest flaw in any technique, he says, "I want to see it corrected, for I've fixed my eyes on the goal. I am living in the now, forgetting the past, so that I can press on toward the future."

Needless to say, there is a need for some good old fashion grit in most of our lives. The Christian life is a great adventure. It is a thrilling experience when we do things for God.

How many things are there in your life that you said you just couldn't do? Well, put them down on a piece of paper: pray over them, and ask God to help you do them. Decide to try and do them with all of your energy and might. And then, what? You know what - go and do them! No pious substitutes: just do them. You have to ask God to give you the strength to do them. He will fulfill his promise! You can bet your life on it.

Determine that you will not continue to drift through life aimlessly. Forget the past, move on toward the goals you set for your life; by lifting your life up with the power of the Almighty One. Become the man or woman that God would have you to be. You will find that life can be exciting in the: "land of beginning again."

EIGHTY EIGHT
We All Have Problems

I heard the story about a small boy who was told by his father, one dark night, to go out and get the broom that was out on the back porch. The boy said: "I'm afraid! It's dark out there." His father replied: "Don't be afraid, son," The Lord's out there and he'll not let anything happen to you." So the little boy went out to the back door, opened it, and looking out into the darkness, shivered and said: "Lord, if you're out there, in the dark, will you please hand me the broom."

The thing we have to remember is that "fear is a given in life." In the epic story "Moby Dick," Captain Ahab declares, "I will have no man on my boat who does not fear the whale." Ahab knew that the fear of things is indeed, in many ways, the beginning of wisdom.

John Mark describes for us, in Chapter four of his Gospel Account, a number of miracles that Jesus accomplished, each of them remembered in detail by Simon Peter. All of them, in the minds of many scholars, are there to impress the reader, with the power inherent in the person of Jesus of Nazareth. Read in the light of the resurrection event, they seem to not be concerned so much with miracles, as they are with the power of the Miracle worker. The suggestion seems to be, if you want to truly combat the fears, the anxieties, and the worries that provoke you along life's way, do it, not by communicating your feelings of panic to God, but by allowing God to communicate his presence and power and their comforting assurance, to you.

The Apostle Paul wrote his friends in Philippi: "Don't worry about anything, but in all your prayers, ask God for what you need, always asking him with a thankful heart. And God's peace, which is far beyond human understanding, will keep your hearts and minds safe, in union with Christ Jesus." (4:6)

I like the story told about several students at Harvard University, years ago. One of them had a terrific personal problem. A roommate suggested that he go and talk to Phillips Brooks. Brooks, the distinguished minister at Trinity Church in Boston (and the writer of the familiar Christmas carol, "O Little Town of Bethlehem) was one of the most famous men of his time. Almost reluctantly the student got in touch with him, and made an appointment.. His friend could hardly wait to hear the report of his visit. "Well, how did it go? Did he solve your problem." The boy responded, "You know, when I was with Dr. Brooks, I forgot I had a problem!"

The most liberating thought that has come down the pike in human history is the thought that the world and every individual in it (and that includes both you and me) are in the hands of God. So, as you look out on the landscape of life; when you begin to worry; when you are ready yo throw in the towel; remember Jesus' words to his disciples, when they were in a boat, on a storm tossing lake: "Why are you so frightened? Do you have no faith?"

The Apostle Paul said it from a layman's point of view: "Don't worry about anything, but (in the presence of any one of your problems) ask God for what you need and God's peace, which is far beyond your understanding, will keep you safe."

Believe it.

EIGHTY NINE

Making Your Life What It Was Intended To Be Like!

I read somewhere that when the English writer J. B. Priestly was asked the question, "Why he had progressed, in his abilities, far in advance of other writers, with the same gifts?" responded, "The difference between us was not in our abilities, but in the fact that they merely toyed with the fascinating idea of writing, I cared like like blazes. And it is this carrying like blazes, that is what counts."

"We need to care like blazes!" It is the subject that the man, we know as Paul, was addressing when he wrote to some of his first century friends, in Corinth, "Run in such a way as to win the prize." New Testament scholars suggest that he was not writing about our being in competition with someone else, but rather, was speaking to them, and now to us, of the necessity of being committed to attaining, for ourselves, "a spiritual excellence." In the original form the words that he wrote were: "Run, that you may lay hold." (I Corinthians 9:24)

He was saying to us, that the individual Christian does not "win," by outdistancing others; they win by "'laying hold:" by holding on tight to God's pattern and purposes for their lives; by the exercise of their gifts and abilities within the range of the responsibility given to them by their God.. Charles Garfield wrote, in his book "Peak Performers" "They are not people with something added, rather they are people with very little of their potential taken away, (read: wasted)." They develop an ability to achieve what they set out to do, and to cultivate, within themselves, the characteristics they value the most. More than any other factor, the differences between them and ordinary performers, is that they consciously, persistently and intelligently refine and develop those characteristics."

"Running to win" involves the possession of a consuming desire to be the best they we can be for Jesus Christ; of determining to explore the farthest reaches of our abilities and to applying them to our spiritual determinations. The only thing we have to remember is that this goal is not achieved easily. It involves giving something up, - so that we have to ask ourselves, "is a personal, intimate relationship with Jesus Christ worth what it might cost me." Run, in such a way, as to win!

Most of us know people who have lost sight of their goals: those whose commitment wavered and was lost. A "finatic," so we are told, is someone who "redoubles their efforts when they get lost." How many of us have forgotten that the central issue in life is not: "what can I do?" but rather, "What do I want to be?" As someone else wrote: "Discipline goes hand in hand with that thought: that is, unless our lives are like arrows shot toward a target, they will have very little impact."

In his book, "The Complete Book Of Running," Jim Fixx describes what he learned about the development of a discipline. "When we race, strange things happen to our minds. The stress of fatigue sometimes makes us forget why we wanted to race in the first place.

In one of my early marathons, (in the middle of the race) I found myself unable to think of a single reason for continuing. Physically and mentally exhausted, I dropped out of the race. Now I won't enter marathon unless I truly want to finish it. So, if during the race I can't remember why I wanted to run, I tell myself, "Maybe I can't remember why I wanted to run now, but I know that I had a good reason when I started."

While I was writing these words, I chanced upon a copy of Bishop Tom Wrights new book of "Daily Readings/Daily Readings For Twenty First Century Christians." It reminded me of the importance of discipline in both the life of the athlete and the Christian disciple. "Running to win," is what the Christian life is all about. It is an all out, every day effort.

Thinking about all you have just read, I wonder, are you engaged daily in the development of your life of discipleship? Do you need to have a Daily Devotional Reading Guide? Do you need to determine to read from the Scriptures, every day?

How about your prayer life? How much do you care about the development of your Christian life? "Do you care like blazes?"

As I said above: "Discipline goes hand in hand with the thought that unless our lives are like arrows, shot toward a target, they will very little impact."

The choice is yours! It's your life! READY! AIM! FIRE!

BIBLIOGRAPHY

I have drawn heavily, and quoted often from the following books

Acuff, Jon: Finish: Give Yourself The Gift Of Done," Penguin, Random House, 2118

Alexander, Claude R. "Necessary Christianity" Intervarsity Press, 2022

Armstrong Karen "A Short History Of Myth" Cannogate

Brogden, Dick "Abiding Mission" (Eugene, OR; Wipf & Stock, 2016)

Christian Century Magazine, October 6, 2021

Covey, Stephen R. "The Seven Habits Of Highly Efficient People Simon Shuster NY, NY 1989

Clear, James "Warren Buffett, "2 List Strategy: How To Maximize Your Focus And Master Your Priorities." James Clear, accessed June 23, 2021 https//Jamesclear. com/buffett - focus

Collier, Winn "A Burning In My Bones" Waterbroo/Penguin/Random House 2021

Cower, Bill "Heart Of Steal" Simon and Shuster, NY, NY

Davis, Pete "Dedicated" Avid Reader Press, New York, New York 2021

Duckworth, Angela "Grit: The Power Of Passion and Perseverance (New York: Scribner 2016)

Edwards, Cliff "Van Gogh's Second Gift" Broadleaf Books, Minneapolis, Minn.

Feller, Bruce "Life In The Transitions" Penguin Press NY, NY

Fixx, Jim "The Complete Book Of Running" Random House, 1970)

Garfield, Charles "Peak Performers" William Morrow Paper Books 1987

Giglio, Louie "Never To Far" Passion Publishing, 2915

Goff, Bob "Love Does" Nelson Books, Nashville, Tenn. 2012

Goff, Bob "UnDistracted" Nelson Books, Nashville, Tenn. 2022

Goff, Bob "Dream Big" Nelson Books 2020

Groeschel, Craig "Winning The War In Your Mind" Zondervan, Grand Rapids, Michigan, 22021

Hamilton, Lee "Words Of Life" Convergent Books New York, NY

Herzog, Maurice "Annapura" Lyon Press 1997

Idelman, Kyle "Gods At War" Zondervan, Grand Rapids, Michigan.

Idelman, Kyle "Don't Give Up" Baker Books Grand Rapids, Michigan

Idelman, Kyle "One At A Time" Baker Books, Grand Rapids, Michigan

Jeremiah, David "Where Do We Go From Here" Thomas Nelson 2021

Jeremiah, David "A Life Beyond Amazing" Thomas Nelson 2017

Jeremiah, David "Forward" Thomas Nelson, 2020

Keller, Timothy "Hope In The Times of Fear" Viking/Random House, NY, NY

Keller, Timothy "Every Good Endeavor" Random House

Keller, Tim "Counterfeit Gods" Penguin Books 2011

Keller/Inazo "Uncommon Ground" Nelson Books, Nashville, Tennessee

Lamott, Anne "Dusk Night Dawn" Riverhead Books, 2021

Larson, Craig Brian "Illustrations For Preaching And Teaching" Baker Books, Grand Rapids, Mich. 1993

Laurie, Greg "Billy Graham: The Man I Knew." Salem Books

Lewis, C. S. "How To Pray" Erdman's/Harper Collins, New York, N.Y. 1967

Luke 22:42-43

Lucado, Max "You Were Made For This Moment" Thomas Nelson 2021

Lucado, Max "Help Is Here" Thomas Nelson, 2022

Lutzer, Erwin W. "We Will Not Be Silenced" Harvest House Publications, Harvest House Publications, Eugene, Oregon 2021

Manresa, Maritsa "Learning To Say NO When You Usually Say Yes" Ocala, FL. Atlantic Publishing Group, 2012

McLaren, Brian "Faith And Doubt" St. Martin Publishing Group. 128 Broadway, NY, NY

Metaxas, Eric "Miracles" Penguin Random House Books New York, New York

Miller, Donald "Blue Like Jazz" Thomas Nelson, Nashville, Tenn.

Nouwin, Henri "Spiritual Direction." Harper-Collins Publishers 2015

Paul, Rand "The Case Against Socialism" Broadside Books, New York, New York

Pederson, Eugene H. "On Living Well" Waterbrook,/Penguin/Random House 2021

Percy, Walker "The Moviegoer"

Peacock, Charlie "A New Way To Be Human: A Provative Look At What It Means To Follow Jesus" Waterbrook Press, Colorado Springs, Colorado 2004

Rohr, Richard "Falling Forward" Jossey-Bass, A Wiley Imprint 2011

Smith, Hannah Witall Smith "Living Confidently In God's Love" Springdale, Pa. Whitaker House. 1984)

Smith, James Bryan "The Good And Beautiful You" Intervarsity Press, 2022

Stanley, Charles "Can You Still Trust God" Nelson Books, Nashville, Tenn. 2021

Stanley, Charles "The Will Of God" Howard Books 2019

Stanley, Andy 'Ask It' "Multinomah Crown Publishing New York 2004/2014

Stanley, Andy "Next Generation Leader" Multanomah Books Random House, NY. NY. 2003

Stowe, Harriet Beecher "Old Town Folks": (Boston and New York: Houghton Mifflin, 1911)

Strobel, Lee "The Case For Heaven" Zondervan Books Grand Rapids, Michigan 2021

Strobel, Lee "The Case For Grace:" Zondervan 2015

Swindoll, Charles, "Clinging To Hope" Tyndale Momentuo 2022

Tozer, A.W. "No Greater Love" Bethany House, Minneapolis, MN

Tozer, A. W. "The Pursuit of God" Bethany House Bloomington, Minn., 2013

Wright, H. Norman "A Better Way To Think," Grand Rapids, Michigan Baker Books, 2011

Wells, Samuel and Hauerwas, Stanley "In Conversation" Church Publishing, New York, NY

Yancey, Philip "Grace Notes" Zondervan, Grand Rapids, Michigan 2009

Youngdahl, Reuben "Turbulent World Tranquil God" OUP

.